BE THE BEST BOSS!

A New Leader's Guide to Success

By Mary Walter

Be The Best Boss!
Published through Mary Walter Leadership, Inc.

ISBN: 978-0-578-50320-2 (Paperback Edition)
ISBN: 978-0-578-50321-9 (Ebook Edition)

For Patrick and Campbell –
You are the joy and the light in my life!

Table of Contents

Preface.. vii

Chapter 1 You're the Leader 1
Learn from the best: Marvin R. Ellison,
President and CEO, Lowe's.. 10

Chapter 2 What Do You Stand For? 15
Learn from the best: Mariana Garavaglia,
Managing Director, Amazon Books... 28

Chapter 3 Hire and Build the Best Team...................................33
Learn from the best: Dave Burwick,
Former CEO, Peet's Coffee & Tea 61

Chapter 4 Deliver Exceptional Results......................................65
Learn from the best: Monika Fahlbusch,
Chief Employee Experience Officer, BMC Software...................... 82

Chapter 5 Create a High-Performance Culture........................87
Learn from the best: Matt Fenlon,
General Manager, MillerCoors.. 109

Chapter 6 Address Poor Performance Directly................... 115
Learn from the best: Shannon Walpole,
Senior Counsel, 24 Hour Fitness 125

Chapter 7 Build a High-Performance Team 129

*Learn from the best: James Clark, President and CEO,
Boys & Girls Clubs of America* 145

Chapter 8 Being Your Own Best Boss 151

*Learn from the best: Keith White, Executive Vice President
of Loss Prevention and Corporate Administration, Gap Inc.* ... 172

References 177

*Your Next Chapter:
Tools and Resources for Your Continued Success* 181

Acknowledgements 185

Preface

S ink or swim.

All too often, new managers are "thrown" into a leadership role and expected to figure out the art of managing others on their own. In a few cases, this "do or die" approach is successful, but most of these new managers do more sinking than swimming, sometimes with heartbreaking, disastrous results.

Making the leap from a skilled individual contributor to a leader is a significant accomplishment. It's a career opportunity offered only to those who have worked extremely hard to prove their worth to the organization. However, these new leaders are disadvantaged without the basic guidance in the art of managing other people. Not only do they make easily avoidable mistakes, but they also waste important opportunities to build their credibility as a leader.

This book is intended to support these new leaders and to help them stay afloat as they get comfortable in their new role. It provides practical tools, advice, and tactics that will help new leaders avoid common leadership dilemmas that prevent them from reaching "Best Boss" status.

First Boss Job

I had two younger sisters, so I often say that my first "boss" job was to manage them. I thought I was great at the job, but I'm sure my sisters would have a different perspective. When I was seventeen, I did get a real, paid leadership job when I was chosen to be the director of the Webelo Aquatics Camp (at the Boy Scout Sea Base) in Newport Beach, California. I had worked at the Sea Base for a couple of years, handing out life jackets and teaching Webelos (ten-year old Boy Scouts) how to canoe and sail.

The Director of the Sea Base, Andy Fitzpatrick, was a true Best Boss. Andy gave me a chance to lead and made me believe I could handle the daily responsibility of managing a team of five instructors (kids my age or younger) and fifty Webelo scouts. I thought it was the perfect job since I didn't seem to have much real responsibility, but a lot of freedom. I soon learned, however, that I was absolutely wrong on the first point.

One day while leading a popular activity in a more remote area of the bay—an area that was just wild enough to allow campers to feel like pirates, and the instructors a reasonable semblance of control—we engaged in an epic Tug of War contest on the beach. It was all fun and games until one of the boys got his arm caught in a twisted section of the rope. The boys pulling from either side made the rope a perfect tourniquet that significantly injured the boy. I raced the boy back to the camp and got him treatment. He suffered no permanent damage (thankfully), but I certainly learned something about the responsibilities of being the boss.

I'm not the perfect leader, nor am I the perfect boss. I've made more than a few mistakes. Luckily, I learned from every mistake and used the experience to become a better leader and a better boss. However, making the same mistakes everyone else makes is just a waste of time; especially when someone is offering to let you learn from their mistakes, so you can forge your own leadership path.

> *You're going to make mistakes, so at least make them interesting!*

My Mission

As a leader, I've made it my mission to study what makes great leaders. I believe that learning from the best is a great shortcut to avoid needless pain and achieve success. I've included one of these *Learn from the Best* interviews at the end of every chapter. These leaders are from a variety of different industries, including GREAT Bosses leading technology companies, non-profit organizations, and retail enterprises. Each leader approaches their leadership role with a unique perspective and brings their own sets of strengths and experiences to the job. You may find some advice that resonates with you, and some that doesn't. I encourage you to approach this book with an open mind and choose the advice that works for you.

Three Key Points

Although I provide a great deal of information and help for new leaders, here are three key points about this book you should remember:

Leadership is a Science

There are real answers to "what makes a great leader." Significant data exists that clarifies how some behaviors and actions strengthen teams and leaders, and other behaviors and actions are counterproductive. You'll find solid research cited in this book to rely on to guide your leadership quest.

Leadership is an Art

Every leader brings a unique set of strengths, style, and approach to the job. Leaders are human beings, and as such, they—just like the rest of us—are constantly changing and evolving; it's a base line requirement for leaders to succeed. You'll find different perspectives in this book, reflecting the myriad ways leaders can succeed.

Leadership is a Craft

Great leaders are made, not born. The behaviors and actions of a Best Boss can be learned. You'll find action items in this book to help you develop your skills and continue a lifelong journey of leadership growth.

How to Use this Book

I was lucky to lead an organization of fifty thousand associates in an expanding company that needed strong leaders to quickly grow into bigger roles. I spent time with newly promoted managers at all levels and was constantly inspired by their commitment, passion, and desire to make a difference. I also noticed that managers tended to struggle in key areas of leadership, like managing conflict, hiring the best team members, delegation, and setting clear goals. Today I serve leaders as a coach, speaker, and team effectiveness guru. This work has given me insight as to what skills and tactics leaders need in order to create unbelievable results through their teams.

This book is not an allegory or an academic exercise. This book is a practical guide to help you become the BEST boss for your team and to help guide your own success as a leader.

Your leadership has a ripple effect on the world around you. Your engaged, happy employees not only deliver results for the company, but also positively affect customers, their friends and family, and the community. My wish for you is that you will experience the tremendous satisfaction and reward that comes with being a Best Boss. Let's get started!

Chapter 1

YOU'RE THE LEADER

IN THIS CHAPTER:
- *How New Leaders Struggle*
- *First Universal Rule*
- *Second Universal Rule*
- *Six Secrets of a Happy Team*
- *Learn from the Best: Advice from Great Leaders*

Congratulations! You are now a leader. Your job performance and clear leadership potential have gotten you here. Now, you have a whole new set of responsibilities and relationships to attend to, including your boss and to those you are charged with leading and ensuring success.

I have spent the bulk of my career leading and helping teams deliver results. It's a job I've always enjoyed, starting with my first job leading teams at the Boy Scout Aquatics Center in Newport Beach, California. As Webelo Day Camp Staff Director, my team led (herded) fifty boys every day toward learning experiences including rowing, canoeing, and sailing. It was an ideal summer job, but it was a terrible leadership training ground for a novice leader. No one in a leadership position seemed to notice the many mistakes I now know I made—except, of course, my staff!

After graduating from college, I stumbled into the retail industry where my degree in political science earned me my first management job, which involved folding jeans all...day...long! Despite such an inauspicious beginning, I stuck with the retail industry and took advantage of the fantastic opportunities I was given to grow as a leader. And as a side benefit, my closet is organized like a Gap store.

In any case, my decision to stay in the retail industry eventually led to much greater responsibility and leadership growth opportunities, including my job as Group Senior Vice President of Stores for a major retailer and direct leadership responsibility for fifty-five thousand employees.

The fast-paced retail business turned out to be a great learning lab for evolving leaders since it provided a daily leadership feedback loop. I got immediate success and failure feedback from my team, and it was these results that guided my growth as a leader; first as a leader in a single large retail store, then as a district manager, a regional manager, and eventually retail sales leadership for an entire organization. Throughout my career, I also had an essential ingredient for every leader's success: access to terrific role models and mentors who gave me advice and guidance to keep my career on track.

> *I want to be a boss*
> *I want to be a big boss*
> *I want to boss the world around*
> *I want to be the biggest boss*
> *That ever bossed the world around*
> *—10cc, "How Dare You"*

How New Leaders Struggle

Although every team I led worked hard to select new leaders who were committed, service-oriented, hardworking, and passionate about delivering results, these leaders often struggled with the same basic leadership transition issues. Yet, when I searched for a resource that would help accelerate this difficult transition period from new leader to expert leader, I came up empty-handed. So, I decided to write my own guidebook.

When I talk to leaders about how well they were prepared to take on a leadership role, what I typically hear is some version of a "sink or swim" story. What a huge waste of time! After all, a great deal of academic research backed up by modern neuroscience and behavioral psychology findings (including the practical experience of successful leaders) clearly demonstrate there are better ways to train new leaders.

The fact is, moving from working to leading without a guide is difficult, if not impossible. Without guidance, new leaders stumble and often fail needlessly when faced with leadership challenges, even those that are easily solved. This book will help you avoid mistakes that will set you back professionally and frustrate you personally. Having seen many leaders make this transition, I've identified the principle secrets to success as well as some common mistakes to avoid. You should use this book as your personal guide to become the Best Boss you can be—beginning on your first day as a new boss!

Why focus on being the Best Boss?

Every leader serves multiple stakeholders: direct reports, peers, bosses, customers, and investors. So why do I recommend focusing and starting with your role as a boss? Because your team enables your success in every other category. A motivated, engaged, and goal-oriented team delivers unbelievable results. Those results (if in line with company goals) will serve your leaders' goals as well. A happy team will serve your customers and create a bond that your competitors can't match. The sales from those loyal customers will create tremendous value for investors. Being a great boss will not only enable your success but will power the success of your team and your organization.

First Universal Rule

This book offers a clear road map to leadership success by offering practical advice and tips at every milepost along the way, from assembling a great team to learning how to relax and enjoy the smoothly running team you have created. But before getting to specifics, here are some universal truths about leading teams, including some personal and expert experiences to make the points crystal clear.

Universal Rule 1 — Your success depends entirely on your team's success.

Terrific performance and loyalty are directly related to your ability to: inspire your team's respect and earn their trust; lead with a service approach; and keep your team's best interest a priority. Here's an example:

One of my proudest moments as a store manager occurred when a customer (she was really a shoplifter attempting to fraudulently return a toaster) threatened to punch me. She was angry and out of control, but I stood my ground even as she took her jacket off to throw her threatened punch. Just in time, twenty employees materialized behind me, and suddenly the refund became less important to this "customer." The point is, I realized that in the most significant ways, my success was completely dependent on my team.

Before this incident, however, my team was anything but cohesive. In fact, it was a very dysfunctional team with a reputation for being notoriously difficult to manage. The team consistently delivered poor results and provoked the ire of customers. When they were not making customers angry, some members spent their time spreading malicious gossip and working to undermine the store's success. Although this problem store was an assignment nobody wanted, I thought I could make a difference, so I took the job. However, I didn't have immediate success with inspiring a new performance direction for the team.

As you can imagine, front line employees in a large retail store spend a lot of time gathering up and re-shelving the inventory that shoppers don't return to the correct rack, bin, or display where they found it. You've probably seen employees in large retail stores doing this work. While some of this is done during the day, most re-shelving work is done after hours, and it is not, to put it mildly, the favorite activity of most employees.

However, motivating the employees at my new assignment to do this task was a particular challenge. Abandoned merchandise was usually piled into empty shopping carts until it could be re-shelved, and on the day I arrived, I discovered thirty-five fully loaded shopping carts of inventory, unprocessed after the previous night's closing. The work was left for the next shift and was a good representation of the lack of execution and accountability in the store's culture. I decided this was a good opportunity to set a new standard, so I rounded up the store's entire front-line team and together we emptied every cart before we went home. I made what I thought was an impressive speech about how we would deliver a better shopping experience for our customers from now on, and I went home that night thinking I made a real difference.

However, when I came back to work the next day, I found thirty-two more equally full shopping carts of inventory waiting to be re-shelved. Although I continued working with the team to change this behavior, nothing I said or did made any difference in motivating the team to change. I had no clue how to fix this miserable environment, and I went home every night frustrated and hopeless.

Help from a Boss

Finally, my boss gave me what now seems an obvious answer: I had the wrong team in place. He completely supported a management team change that put the right people in the right positions to help me succeed. I used that mandate to create the following team:

- Gary, Operations Executive Leader – Gary had years of retail experience and had a long record of getting results.
- Stephen, Merchandising Executive Leader – Stephen was terrific at his job, and he kept smiling no matter what happened. He built valuable relationships with the entire store staff.
- Brian, Merchandise Executive Leader – Brian was whip-smart, and he had a real talent at developing plans that could fix any problem.
- Bobby, Apparel Executive Leader – Bobby was a fabulous merchandising expert and team-builder.

- Nicole, Customer Service Leader – Nicole was a sincere, authentic professional who created a contagious commitment to our customers among the front-line staff.

I brought the new team together with clear goals and expectations and provided a detailed road map on how we would work together to deliver results. The new team transformed the store's operations. In fact, the store eventually delivered the district's best sales performance, best customer service improvement ratings, and best profitability in the region. It was the team's exemplary performance that led to both my next promotion and the advancement of the other team leaders. The lesson here is clear: A great team is always critical to everyone's success!

Universal Rule 2 – If you want your team to get behind you, you must first get behind them.

People choose to follow their leader. The child's game of "Follow the Leader" only works as a preschool game. In the real world, expecting people to line up behind you because you've been designated their leader is a recipe for disaster. You must give those you lead a reason to work for you, including the all-important employee reason for following a leader: WIIFM (What's in it for me?).

Exercise – Best Boss Aspirations

Here's an exercise to help you begin developing your essential leadership skills. Read the following questions and jot down your answers in the space provided below or on a separate piece of paper.

What do you want in a boss?

Answering this question will help you gain clarity and empathy for what motivates and engages those you now lead. Be specific, and consider both intangible ("Does the boss care about me as a person?") and tangible ("Does the boss meet with me to discuss my career goals?") aspects of the question.

Once you've created this Best Boss aspirational list, post it somewhere you'll often see it. Delivering on these top line expectations will help you serve your team and ensure your own success and the team's success.

My Ideal Boss:

- _____
- _____
- _____
- _____
- _____
- _____
- _____

Six Secrets of a Happy Team

Throughout this book, I'll provide practical tips for achieving new leader success, but here are some basic "rules of the road" that will help you to be the Best Boss you can be.

- **Communicate, communicate, communicate!** – Teams look to you for direction, advice, information, and encouragement. The Best Boss shares information openly, consistently and quickly. Keeping your team informed reduces rumors, misunderstandings, and helps your team to make good decisions.

- **Set clear goals and expectations** – Make your criteria for success an "open book test." You need to be clear about what success looks like if you expect to lead a winning team.
- **Be Vulnerable** – Let the team know your strengths and goals as well as your personal struggles and joys. Enlist their help to achieve your goals, as you will work to help them. Your willingness to share openly will create an atmosphere where your team will share as well.
- **Build trust** – Confidence is built when you always do what you say you will do. Building trust also means never speaking negatively of others when they are absent.
- **Remove obstacles** – Provide the necessary resources to help those you lead solve problems and be resilient.
- **Build a great team** – Add only solid performers to your team. Don't allow poor performers to impact the work of your team.

Finally, as a new leader, you *will* make mistakes! It is part of the job so don't be afraid to take chances. It makes you a more interesting leader, and these mistakes will often teach you much more than your successes do.

Learn from the Best: Advice from Great Leaders

Being a great boss requires commitment not only to your team, but also to your personal growth. Listening to successful leaders accelerates our success by allowing us to learn from their experiences. I've asked the same questions in each of these interviews to demonstrate the many paths to great leadership.

Marvin R. Ellison, President and CEO, Lowe's

Marvin Ellison thinks of himself as the "Motivator In Chief." He says that he feels it is his responsibility to engage associates, to make them feel special, listen to their concerns, help them solve problems, and then give them the leadership they need to make them successful. Marvin says, "I lead my team in the art of the possible."

Marvin Ellison has served as president and chief executive officer of Lowe's Companies, Inc. since July 2018, when he also joined Lowe's board of directors. He most recently served as chairman and CEO of J.C. Penney Company Inc., where he implemented a turnaround strategy that improved the company's balance sheet, increased store productivity, optimized operations, and grew key categories.

Ellison earned a bachelor's degree in business administration from the University of Memphis and an MBA from Emory University. He serves on the boards of FedEx Corporation, the Retail Industry Leaders Association, and the National Retail Federation. He also serves as a member of the board of trustees for the University of Memphis. Ellison was named to Fortune's World's Greatest Leaders in 2016 and was recognized as the 2016 Corporate Executive of the Year by Black Enterprise.

What quality do you think is critical to be a great boss?

Being a great listener. It's simple, but very important. My mother always said that God gave us two ears and one mouth for a reason. Understand people as individuals and show them that you are interested in their career aspirations and goals.

What mistakes do you see new leaders make?

They think they must have all the answers. This belief forces people to not use their resources, to miss delegating, and to demonstrate a lack of humility. Admitting what you don't know creates "followship;" people see you as authentic. You create a safe environment for your followers to admit what they don't know, so everyone can grow.

What advice would you give yourself in your first management job?

Have more intellectual curiosity. As I look back, I did enough in my job, but I didn't take initiative to learn everything around me. I focused on doing what was expected in my job. I've since learned the importance of understanding how the components in the company connect with each other, how all the aspects of the retail operations, from the cashier registers to the back room, work together to deliver.

What advice do you have to address employee performance issues?

There are two areas to consider when addressing performance issues:

1. When you don't deal with poor performance, you send a message to the rest of the team. You send a message to the high performers that what they're doing is not important. This is a silent and deadly message to send.

2. When you have someone who is failing, look at it as a rescue mission. They are either in the wrong job, or they need to perform better. They didn't join to fail, so consider how you can rescue by either training and

developing or help them move to a new role where they are better suited to succeed.

Do you have a favorite interview question that helps you hire great people?

One of my favorite interview questions is, "Give me two to three people that you've developed in your career that you're most proud of." Leaders can always answer quickly and with a lot of passion; it separates out a strong individual performer from someone who can build talent for the future. It is all about the people!

How do you stay healthy in this job?

Spiritual Health: I never apologize for having a strong faith in God and commitment to my faith. My spiritual health allows me not to be stressed out day to day; I'm committed to a higher purpose. If I'm doing the right things and following the plan, the results will be the best outcome for the long term. My focus is about the people I put in place and commitment to the strategy, not day-to-day results. This means that I don't carry a lot of stress; I sleep well at night!

Physical health: I set a good routine; working out, getting appropriate rest, and eating well on a consistent basis.

My spiritual focus makes up about 80 percent of my well-being, the physical 20 percent. It's important to be a whole person, to have a good home life that gives you meaning and happiness.

What's Next

In the next chapter, you'll learn how to create a rock-solid foundation for your team's success that is built on your values.

Your team is wondering what you stand for and what kind of leader they can expect. Give them something good to talk about!

Chapter 2

WHAT DO YOU STAND FOR?

IN THIS CHAPTER:
- *Three Key Value Considerations*
- *Company Values and Priorities*
- *Personal Values and Codes of Conduct*
- *Values Exercise*
- *Real World Translation*
- *Clarifying Exercise*
- *Learn from the Best*

Your hard work and clear line of sight to your core values were two key attributes that helped you win your new leadership role. Congratulations! Now, your team expects you to provide both the performance and behavioral expectations that they will use as guardrails to guide their own success. While it is true that almost everyone follows a broad set of personal and professional values (fairness, honesty, trustworthiness), leaders are expected to dig even deeper and fully understand and define the personal value system that will guide them toward being the Best Boss they can be.

When your values are clear to you, making decisions
becomes easier.
—Roy E. Disney

The Importance of Values-Based Leadership

One of the most common mistakes new leaders make is focusing exclusively on expectations while ignoring the values that drive their strategy or vision. This "just do it" approach may work for the short term, but is not very effective in creating an engaged, committed team. A far better way to rally your team's support is to focus first on the values that inform and guide your leadership style and approach. Save the specifics—including job performance and business tactics—until later. Remember, leaders are responsible for leading both the long and short game. Connecting your vision to a solid set of personal (and by extension, shared) values is the best way to build support among your team. You'll be answering the most important question that team members are likely to have during their initial interactions with you: "What kind of boss will she/he be?"

Defining values for yourself and your team begins to create a place to work that holds meaning and importance outside the extrinsic rewards of pay. We all want to work somewhere that aligns with our values and to do work that feels important. The management consulting company Deloitte demonstrated the importance of values among millennial employees (1). In a survey covering thirty-six countries and over ten thousand millennial employees, they found that only 48 percent of respondents believe businesses behave ethically, and 47 percent believe that business leaders are committed to helping improve society. If you behave ethically and demonstrate commitment to higher values, you will have an incredible advantage! People will want to work harder for you if they know they are supporting work that is worthy of their commitment.

Three Key Value Building Considerations

In general, there are at least three key factors to consider when building a values-based approach to team leadership.

- Company Values and Priorities
- Personal Values and Codes of Conduct
- Real World Translation

Some companies bake their operational and behavioral values into every external and internal communication. Other companies are less consistent about pushing their employees to align the work they do to these values. Still, just about every company of every size follows at least implicitly—and most, specifically—a defined set of standards. Aligning yourself with these values helps ensure a positive start as a team leader. The specifics of your own plan should be directly tied to these values and how this linkage benefits both your team members and the company that pays their wages. The section that follows explores these three key leadership factors.

Company Values and Priorities

Understanding your company's implicit and explicit values is the first step toward building a values-based leadership approach. As noted, all companies to a greater or lesser degree spend a considerable amount of time defining these values, and they are usually expressed in a mission or vision statement. These declarations specifically state how these values impact their employees, the immediate and worldwide community in which the company operates, and the return their shareholders can expect to receive from their investment.

Some companies absolutely abide by these statements while others, often to their detriment, lose their commitment to their core values over time. That's why the best companies revisit these statements often to ensure relevancy and meaning to their business. You can easily find examples of these statements through internet searches, but consider this simple values/mission statement from L.L.Bean displayed prominently on its website (2).

> **L.L.'s Golden Rule**
> *"Sell good merchandise at a reasonable profit, treat your customers like human beings and they will always come back for more."*
> —Leon Leonwood Bean

This "Golden Rule" is further explained at some length, but this is the core, bottom-line value that clearly drives the company's operations.

With L.L.Bean's mission/vision statement in mind, think about how you might answer these questions:

- If you were a manager L.L.Bean, what activity or behavior would likely bring success?
- What would get you fired?
- What other values, not stated specifically, do you think would be important to the company?

We can assume that a leader working at L.L.Bean would be rewarded for great customer service. Likewise, ignoring customer complaints or disrespecting customers would surely lead to negative consequences.

What about quality? Would cutting corners on customer quality to meet a budget be acceptable? If your company is guided by a strong mission statement, the leaders within it will have answers to those questions. A boss is responsible for leading their team through competing priorities. You'll need to decide where to focus and what is most important. Your values, and the values of the company, should be your top priority. If you stay true to them, you'll never compromise your integrity.

Here's another good example to consider—Nordstrom's Mission Statement:

*In our store or online, wherever new opportunities arise-Nordstrom works relentlessly to give customers the most compelling shopping experience possible. The one constant? John W. Nordstrom's founding philosophy: offer the customer the best possible **service**, **selection**, **quality** and **value**. (3)*

Imagine you are a leader at this company. How might this mission statement guide your priorities? Would you place your focus on the customer, or saving the company money? What behavior would you reward from your team members? Would you forgive a policy violation if it was done in service to a customer? Using this mission statement as a guide, bosses have a clear view of company priorities, and are able to make decisions to support the company's values and goals.

The Nordstrom mission statement provides clear direction on company values and priorities. But not all mission statements are this clear. The company Life Is Good has a very short, expansive mission statement: "Spreading the Power of Optimism" (4). Now imagine yourself as a leader at this company. Does it make you smile? This statement feels good and creates a feeling that your work is bigger than your job. But does this statement give you enough information to determine what is most important? Could you make decisions based on this statement? For example, if you were forced to make a trade-off between quality and meeting your budget targets, what would you do? Clearly, you'd need more information.

So, what's the point? To be a truly great boss you must have complete clarity on both your company's values and priorities, and your own. I knew a retail leader who would say, "Missing the payroll budget will get you in trouble, but having a bad looking store will get you fired." He was brilliantly articulating that company's values: sales and customers were more important than meeting short-term financial goals. Understanding your company's values and priorities can make the difference between success for you and your team, and failure.

Company Values and Priorities Exercise

Here's a quick exercise that will guide you in discovering your company's values and priorities:

Step One: Gather Data

Become a student of your own company and research its values and priorities, even if you're a long-time employee. Great sources of this information include:

- Annual reports (the best place to find mission and values statements)
- Employee handbooks and training materials
- Performance review criteria

Step Two: Define Values and Priorities

You will likely find far too much information in Step One! Create a narrow set of priorities that you can use to guide your actions and lead your team. Answer these questions to narrow your list:

- What are the top two values for the company? For example, quality, customer service, or community service.
- What are the top priorities for the company? These may include growth, sales, or improving the customer experience.
- What are two or three values that are not important to the company? Having this information will help you

know what you should avoid; don't waste your time being great at something that is not valued!

Step Three: Verify

You now have a clear idea of what is most important to your company, and by extension, to your team. Because this information is so critical to your success, check your assumptions. Share this list with your boss or a mentor, and make sure you're in agreement.

Personal Values and Codes of Conduct

The second consideration in a values-based leadership approach is understanding and then firmly establishing your own personal set of values and an expected code of conduct. This section will help you with this task, beginning with a simple thought exercise. Think about these questions below; note the answers on another piece of paper or on your computer, if you wish.

- What's most important to you?
- What got you here?
- What do you value in others?
- What values are non-negotiable?

If you're like most new leaders, just thinking through (or jotting down) the answers likely creates quite a long list. That's good. You have clearly defined values. However, you can't stand for everything, so you'll have to narrow down your list and make choices. Otherwise, you'll confuse your team with too many choices. This exercise will help you decide what's most important.

Values Exercise

Use this exercise as a filtering tool. Here are the directions in three steps:

STEP 1 – Review this list of values below (see Figure 2.1), and check the values you believe are most important. This filtering work won't be easy since your choices are limited to ten values.

Some of the values you might hold dear personally, but remember, this is for the workplace, so these values might not be appropriate. Leaving out a personal value doesn't mean you're being dishonest, it just means there's a time and place for everything.

For example, if you are deeply religious, you may find that faith is your number one personal value. However, since your team members may not share your religious beliefs, it is best to keep this value to yourself. You may find other values that align with your faith and your work, such as kindness, empathy, or service. Shifting focus will ensure that everyone on your team will feel accepted while you remain true to your values.

Note that you should feel free to add to the list if you don't see a word that reflects your values. However, that doesn't change the requirement to limit your value choices to ten.

- O Achievement
- O Accuracy
- O Authenticity
- O Balance
- O Beauty
- O Boldness
- O Change
- O Calm
- O Challenge
- O Collaboration
- O Community
- O Compassion
- O Confidence
- O Contentment
- O Contribution
- O Cooperation
- O Courage
- O Creativity
- O Curiosity
- O Delivering Results
- O Determination
- O Direct communication
- O Diversity
- O Empathy
- O Empowerment
- O Enthusiasm
- O Excellence
- O Fairness
- O Family
- O Flexibility
- O Forgiveness
- O Freedom
- O Friendship
- O Fun Generosity
- O Gratitude
- O Grit

- O Happiness
- O Hard Work
- O Health
- O Honesty
- O Honor
- O Humor
- O Inclusion
- O Independence
- O Innovation
- O Integrity
- O Kindness
- O Learning
- O Love
- O Loyalty
- O Optimism
- O Organization
- O Participation
- O Passion
- O Patience
- O Peace
- O Personal Growth
- O Praise
- O Problem Solving
- O Productivity
- O Respect
- O Safety
- O Self-Control
- O Service to others
- O Simplicity
- O Spirituality
- O Spontaneity
- O Strength
- O Teamwork
- O Tact
- O Tolerance
- O Tradition
- O Wealth

Figure 2.1

STEP 2 – Now, go back and look at the list. Are there any values that are truly non-negotiable to you? What values, if lacking, would cause you to fire someone? Make sure these are on your list.

STEP 3 – Narrow your list to only three values. This can be challenging, because each of these values may seem extremely important to you. One way to break a tie is to ask yourself, "What does this value look like at work? How does that translate to results?" Rank ordering your list will help you determine what is most important.

When you're done, your values list should look something like this sample one below:

<u>***My list of values:***</u>
Integrity and honesty
Service to others
Delivering results

Real World Translation

Of course, values are fine, but businesses still operate in the real world and must report tangible investment returns to be successful. This next section will help you with this task.

So, what does integrity really mean in a "real world" context? What definition of integrity is acceptable, and where do you draw the line? These internal discussions are key to how you set boundaries for both your behavior and those you lead.

Translating your values list into the "real world" also means figuring out how to combine your personal values and those espoused by your company. By doing this work now you'll be mapping out a clearly articulated path ahead for yourself and your team.

Clarifying Exercise

This exercise will help you to clarify your thinking so that your team is clear on your expectations. Leaders sometimes assume that everyone shares their values or understands the consequences for violating them. If an employee is completely surprised by their failure to live up to what you believe is an established value or expectation, then you have failed them as a leader. Here is a personal example:

Our store café had a strict and clearly stated policy that everyone must pay for the food served at the restaurant; this policy included friends, family, or other employees. Violators of this policy were terminated in all cases. Despite this clearly articulated rule and the severe consequences for not following it, I had an employee who gave a friend a free meal. When the employee was confronted about the incident, she did not deny her actions and was surprised about both the strict rule and the consequences for ignoring it. Unfortunately, the employee lost her job, which was a tough learning experience for both the jobless employee and for me as the leader, forced to lose an employee whom I valued. Clarity of consequences is sometimes the kindest act of a great boss!

Creating a Values Statement

STEP 1 – Write a few sentences that describe the behaviors you might expect to be the result of each value, including any conflicting values you can imagine. Here are a few examples:

- **Collaboration:** *We share updates on our projects during our weekly meetings and provide honest input and feedback. We never speak negatively of a peer to others; we are loyal to the absent.*
- **Delivering Results:** *We achieve every budget line; we don't sacrifice meeting expenses in the pursuit of sales.*
- **Customer Service:** *We will do everything in our power to make the customer happy; we will break rules to serve our customer; we will never let a customer leave unhappy.*
- **Integrity:** *We always act in the best interest of the company and our team. If we need to violate a rule to satisfy a customer, we involve a partner to ensure we're not sacrificing long-term integrity for short-term gain.*

You can see that each of these statements enable employees to make decisions while staying aligned to the values important to the company. These statements also provide clear guidance on priorities, and let the team know what is most important.

Avoid This Mistake!

As you craft your message, be careful of straying too far from the company mission and values. Your success, and that of your team, depends on your alignment with the company's priorities. It is better to repeat these messages to ensure you are on the right path than to create your own message that gets your team off track.

STEP 2 – Write a brief statement that expresses your values and why they are important to you and the team you lead.

Value: Why it's important: What it looks like in practice:

_____

_____

_____

_____

_____

You now have your foundation for success! Your team will appreciate your clarity and the clear directions. By providing this guidance, you are making it easier to make the right decisions to ensure success for both you and your team. And you're well on your way to becoming the Best Boss!

Learn from the Best: Advice from Great Leaders

Being a great boss requires commitment not only to your team, but also to your personal growth. Listening to successful leaders accelerates our success by allowing us to learn from their experiences. I've asked the same questions in these interviews to demonstrate the many paths to great leadership.

Mariana Garavaglia, Director,
Head of Store Management, Amazon Books

Mariana has led the successful launch of Amazon Books, bringing the Amazon experience to life for customers across the United States. Prior to this role, Mariana held numerous operational and HR positions at Amazon, including serving as Country HR Manager for Spain. Mariana is fluent in Spanish and English, holds an MBA from the Tuck School of Business at Dartmouth, and a BA from the University of Oklahoma.

What quality do you think is critical to be a great boss?

One of the principles we have at Amazon is "Learn & Be Curious." It states that leaders are never done learning and always seek to improve. I think one of the key things critical to being a great boss is applying that idea of continuous improvement to your work and your team's work. It's so important to create an environment of thoughtful feedback, a willingness to openly address and learn from mistakes, and a culture of learning and curiosity.

What mistakes do you see new leaders make?

There are two things I commonly see with new leaders, and they are two sides of the same coin. The first is what I call the Super Individual Contributor approach. These new leaders amplify what they were doing before as individual contributors and just do more of the same. They take on too many things directly, don't leverage and expand ownership to their teams, and have a difficult time scaling and getting the most out of their team. On the flip side, some new leaders very quickly "let go" of things and delegate too much without having great check-in mechanisms.

As you start to delegate some of the work you used to do directly, as more of the work you accomplish is done through guiding and directing others, much of your success will come from your ability to help prioritize and guide your team. You'll have to expand your breadth of focus. But as you do this, it's important to establish the right mechanisms that will also allow you to dive deep. It's super frustrating for teams to have a boss who doesn't really understand their work or who is out of touch with the details of how their teams are operating. You should think about these key questions as you prepare for your new role: How will you both scale and stay connected to the details? What will be the ways in which you will audit and maintain a pulse of the work that is happening on the front line? It's important to stay connected to the details, not to micromanage, but to understand and to drive consistency, accountability, and thoughtful prioritization.

If you had advice for yourself in your first management role, what would it be?

You don't have to solve everything at once. But you do have to prioritize and pick a couple of key things that you are going to tackle; and you do have to communicate those priorities thoughtfully and consistently to your team. Create a strong vision of what you want the future state to look like, and outline the steps for how you will programmatically get there.

What do you think makes a boss great?

Knowing what motivates their team, understanding how to adjust their style to meet their team's needs. Asking lots of questions. Seeking to understand. Knowing what motivates and inspires each of your team members.

Do you have any secrets for building a great team?

Set a high bar. Great teams will want to rise to meet it. Hire people that you are proud of. Hire people that can grow to do your job—ideally, better than you can. Hire people that you can look at a couple of years down the road and say, "Yes, that person was a truly great hire." This takes time, and when you have open positions that you need to fill, it's sometimes tempting to hire quickly and just fill the role. Don't compromise long-term decisions to address a short-term pain-point. Be patient; hire thoughtfully and hire for the future. Hiring is one of the most important things you do as a leader, and great hires will be your most enduring legacy.

How do you stay healthy while doing this job?

Something people don't talk a lot about is sleep health, but more than a third of Americans don't get enough sleep on a regular basis, and according to studies heavy cell phone users are the most sleep deprived. One simple thing I do is leave my cell phone in the kitchen. I use an old-fashioned alarm clock or Alexa to wake up in the morning, and not having your cell phone in your room means you won't be tempted to check in if you're tossing or turning at night. I had a boss once who would send emails at two or three a.m. Unless you're in a job that has on-call rotations, for which you should have established practices and clear mechanisms, there are no emails that need to be sent at two a.m. that can't wait until the next morning. And sending messages at these hours sets an untenable and unfair expectation for your team.

What advice do you have to address employee performance issues?

First and foremost, don't be afraid to have honest and frank conversations with your employee—and address issues early. Also, assume positive intent. Few people come into work thinking, "Today I'm going to do a terrible job." If you have an employee that is not performing, seek to understand what is preventing them from doing their job, ensure they know what the expectations of the job are, and have frank conversations with them about what success in their role looks like.

Do you have a favorite interview question that helps you hire great people? How do you hire?

Humility, self-awareness, and a willingness to be vocally self-critical are things that are important to assess during the interview process and are difficult to coach. I like to ask people how they have evolved and improved over the last year or two. I tend to ask, "How are you better today than you were a couple of years ago? What areas have you been trying to improve or work on?"

What's Next

In the next chapter, we'll focus on perhaps the most important task of a great boss: hiring a terrific team. Being the Best Boss means creating a team of talented players. Your team is counting on you to build a team that makes everyone better and delivers results. How do you make that happen? Read on to find out!

Chapter 3

HIRE AND BUILD THE BEST TEAM

IN THIS CHAPTER:
- *Building Your Best Team*
- *Avoiding Bias*
- *Authentic and Effective Interviewing*
- *Your Most Important Decision*
- *Learn From the Best*

One of the most important jobs of every leader or manager is building a great team. It's nearly impossible to deliver the results your organization expects without an exceptional team to help you toward that goal. This chapter provides all the basic information you'll need to build a new team and offers some guidance on how to avoid classic team building mistakes many leaders make during the hiring process.

"I noticed that the dynamic range between what an average person could accomplish and what the best person could accomplish was 50 or 100 to 1. Given that,

> *you're well advised to go after the cream of the cream. A small team of A+ players can run circles around a giant team of B and C players."*
> —Steve Jobs

Building Your Best Team

Despite the inherent complexity of the topic, the process of building a great team involves three essential activities:

- Deciding Whom to Interview
- Asking the Right Questions
- Choosing the Best Candidate

Yes, it's true a universe of complexity is represented within these three bullet points; but it's also true that no matter how detailed the process or methodology you use, hiring is mostly a matter of a leader's ability to do three things: spot the best potential performers who can get along with other team members (i.e. avoid bullies or prima donnas, for example); determine a potential team member's commitment to ethical behavior; and judging if a candidate will fully support you, your team, and the organization that employs them. That's why *hiring is **THE** most important thing you do as a manger!*

If you take the time to hire team members who are results-focused, treat others with respect, are open to feedback, and strive to delight customers, your life as a leader will be a lot more enjoyable. However, if you hire team members who avoid responsibility and take shortcuts, gossip behind other team member's backs, and irritate your customers, life as a leader will be nothing short of a living hell. The choice seems clear.

About the Interview Process

Every potential new hire deserves a fair hearing, but at the same time leaders have a responsibility to hire only candidates they feel confident will succeed and perhaps just as important, will be a good fit for their team. That's why you can't afford to let your own personal biases cloud the choices you make during the hiring process.

Owning up to our personal biases is difficult. But the fact is, we all bring both conscious and unconscious biases to the workplace despite our best intentions. Conscious biases—those that we can all easily identify, such as preferring one flavor of ice cream or another—are not difficult to leave at the door. Unconscious biases—including ethnicity, race, sexual orientation, or body type biases—are harder to admit, and they influence the decisions we make.

The problem is that humans naturally gravitate toward people we personally identify with; i.e., those people who share our own background (small town origins, for example), race, or gender. Even a person's choice of coffee over tea can color our impression of someone we're interviewing. As a new leader, pay close attention to these biases when building your BEST team. Why? Bias may lead you to select a candidate based on something that has nothing to do with future success ("We went to the same High School!") and a new employee who may end up being an employee that you eventually need to terminate. Bias may also lead you to eliminate a candidate for reasons that have nothing to do with their ability to perform, and the potential to let terrific talent go to the competition. To help you consider your sensitivity about bias, consider how you might answer these questions:

- What are your most frequently triggered conscious biases?
- Are you able to identify any potential unconscious biases?
- What hidden bias do you think might influence your hiring decisions?

Of course, just thinking about these questions on your own is more a thought exercise than anything else since we all have different ways to measure and minimize our biases. That's why it's important to dig a little deeper.

An Example of Bias at the NBA

Does unconscious bias affect our decisions? A study of bias among National Basketball Association (NBA) referees conducted between 1991 and 2002 by Joseph Price and Justin Wolfers, professors at Brigham Young University and the University of Pennsylvania, found that more personal fouls were awarded against players when they were officiated by an opposite-race refereeing crew than when they are officiated by an own-race refereeing crew. The study concluded that these biases were sufficiently large and affected the outcome of an appreciable number of games. (Note that the results did not distinguish whether the bias stems from the actions of white or black referees.) (5)

Curious to see if the bias continued, Professor Devin G. Pope from the University of Chicago reviewed the time after the NBA referees learned of the bias results (2003-2006), and after widespread publicity of the study had occurred (2007-2010). This review found the bias continued in the first three-year period after the study but that no bias was apparent after the widespread publicity of the first study's findings were released during the second three-year period.

The NBA did not take any specific action to eliminate referee discrimination after the initial study or to change referee incentives and training. (6) The researchers concluded media exposure alone was apparently enough to bring about the attitude change and the subsequent increase in fairness among NBA referees. Clearly, awareness of unconscious bias (and perhaps social pressure to do the right thing) can lead to more equitable decisions.

Luckily, it's not that difficult to find help in identifying your hidden biases and to minimize their impact on your hiring decisions. One tool that can help leaders identify personal bias is the implicit association test developed by Project Implicit®. This free online survey was developed by a group of leading academics committed to studying implicit bias. You can find the tool at this website: https://implicit.harvard.edu/implicit/.

You cannot be the Best Boss without the best team. Your ability to find, recruit, and promote is key to your success, and the success of your team. The Best Boss will find those great players who may be hidden from other, less aware leaders due to personal bias.

One final note on the problem posed by allowing bias to impact your hiring decisions: If you hire only people who are similar, you'll miss critical opportunities to find solutions that might never occur to a team of clones. And, as every leader knows, it is often a company's ability to "see problems differently" that ultimately separates organizations from their competition.

Step 1: Deciding Whom to Interview

Your first task as a leader is to carefully review the resumes or applications of potential candidates. Resumes are packed with important clues to help you assess whom to interview. Here are some details that I focus on during this important first step:

- **Does the candidate's resume or application contain errors?** This might seem an obvious requirement, but if the candidate glosses over these details you must question their ability to be diligent as an employee.
- **Does the candidate's resume include any accomplishments that indicate a commitment to results and not just responsibilities?** For example, was the candidate responsible for verifiable performance indicators, such as meeting sales goals or production quotas? What you're looking for here is not just what the candidate's role entailed but how they performed that role. You're looking for clues that this person can become a team member who will deliver not just on expectations but will make your team exceptional. Look for indications that they exceeded results, not just performed a job. You're looking for employees who will act like owners. These team members are few and far between, but they can make all the difference in your success. Your resume screen is a good spot to find the extra level of effort that

will help you identify an exceptional employee. If you're hiring entry-level employees, the resumes may or may not be very detailed or have results-oriented claims. However, if you are hiring a new manager for your team, the resumes you'll review will most likely include such performance data, which makes a resume a terrific tool to assess potential.

Here's an exercise to make this point: Imagine you're hiring someone to manage a team of cashiers in a grocery store. Which of these resumes would you choose?

Yes!	Not so great
Improved customer service survey scores by 15% by implementing new recognition program for cashiers	Responsible for supervising cashier team
Responded to every customer complaint within 24 hours, the fastest response time in the company	Handled customer complaints
Reduced absenteeism by 24% by allowing shift sharing, which was subsequently adopted as a company-wide solution	Managed attendance
Educated peers on customer service priorities; conducted role play exercise to improve consistency of manager's response to complaints	Served as a member of the management team
Improved cash shortage by $11,000 for the year by following up with daily cashier shortage reports	Responsible for cash handling

Figure 3.1

It is difficult to hold out for the "A" candidate, so that's why you should be proactive and interview potential candidates before you have an opening. That's the best way to ensure that you'll hire someone who will truly contribute to your team. After all, there are far more candidates who are just looking to do a job than candidates who really want to make a difference. If you want to be the Best Boss to your team, you've got to have the courage to wait for the candidate that meets your high standards and one who will make your team even better. (More on finding great talent in Chapter Four).

- **How long did the candidate work at their previous job?** If a candidate changes jobs frequently, such lack of stability requires an explanation. Many reasonable explanations exist (for example, financial problems of former employers or moving with a spouse to another city), but frequent moves can indicate a problem. If you do decide to interview a candidate with a history of job-skipping, make sure to devote enough time during the conversation to decide if this candidate will stick with you. Asking "why" is the easiest way to identify the real root cause and help you understand the candidate's values and motivations for changing jobs. Take this conversation for example:

"Why did you leave your role at Ajax?"
"I was recruited for a better opportunity at Boxu."
"Why was the opportunity better?"
"I liked the environment better."
"What did you like about the environment?"
"Well, my boss at Ajax was a real jerk. He was so demanding and didn't cut me any slack when I was late."

You'll notice quite a few questions were required to get to the clue about future performance. (Be forewarned: any candidate who openly criticizes a prior boss is likely to do the same to you.) Identifying the reasons why a candidate has transitioned between jobs is critical. You may find a pattern that indicates positive reasons such as upward movement and career growth; or you might discover the candidate avoids difficulty by quitting. The resume review is your opportunity to find clues that will lead you to explore further or move on to another candidate. The next chapter covers the many ways to identify qualified candidates.

Step Two: Asking the Right Questions

Once you've selected a group of qualified candidates, the next step is a face-to-face meeting. It's here that you begin to get a solid understanding of a potential candidate, including their strengths, weaknesses, work ethic, and ability to collaborate with other team members. Divining this information requires putting the candidate at ease so that they feel comfortable letting down natural barriers to transparency with strangers, not to mention the barriers that the interview process naturally creates.

Some leaders believe keeping the candidate "on edge" is the best way to get the information needed to make a hiring decision; some are even proud of their reputation as a difficult interviewer. Personally, I think this method has more to do with ego and is not a particularly effective approach. Nervousness and fear do not create transparency, and you won't find out much by scaring an interviewee to death.

If a candidate is at ease, they will be more likely to share their proudest accomplishments, their true work habits, or a personal passion that reveals an important aspect of their personality. If the candidate leaves a job interview feeling that the interviewer didn't really "get" them, then that's a sure sign that the experience was a waste for both parties; and sadly, perhaps a lost opportunity for your organization.

Here are some tips that will help you put job candidates at ease. The best way to create an environment of trust that enables authenticity is to demonstrate it. Be yourself—the candidate deserves to know what you're like as a boss as much as you deserve to know what they're like as an employee.

Tips for Putting Candidates at Ease

- Start with a smile and a handshake. You'd be surprised how many bosses remain seated when a candidate arrives (a great strategy if you want your candidate to decide they wouldn't want to work with you).
- Begin your interview with easy small talk. The goal is to let them know you're not an ogre and that you truly want to get to know them!
- Your first question should focus on a candidate's past successes. After all, you've seen their resume and something in it has impressed you enough to ask them in for an interview, so ask them about it. You'll not only put them at ease, you'll learn about their passion, their drive, and how they accomplish results.

Team Interviewing

Whole Foods Market has been recognized on *Fortune Magazine*'s prestigious Great Places to Work list for eighteen consecutive years. (7) The company takes a unique approach to hiring with a commitment to its current team members that new additions will be a great match. Team members participate in interviews for all leadership positions; as the company states, "Team member participation in group interviews is one way we put our culture of empowerment into action. The team interview process is an effective way to make hiring decisions because the diversity of participants brings all the different aspects of the roles and responsibilities of the position to the table. In addition, the process educates both the interviewers and the candidates by giving insight into all the expectations and challenges of the job." (8) Involving your team in your interviews is a terrific way to be their Best Boss and to hire the best people!

Authentic and Effective Interviewing

Some leaders like to ask difficult, or even trick questions to help them determine the fitness of a potential candidate. Research has demonstrated that this approach is ineffective in identifying an employee who will be successful. It is far better to focus on what I believe is the most important factor in hiring: *the best predictor of future performance and behavior is past performance and behavior.* Interviewers are like investigators, probing to identify the truth that is often hidden behind artifice and nerves. You want to know not only how this candidate will perform, you also want to know about their values.

Fortunately, you don't have to rely exclusively on what a candidate says or just their resume. As F. Scott Fitzgerald said, "Action is character." (9) I would make this addition to this iconic author's maxim: "Our past actions predict our future actions." We all grow and make mistakes, but when looking for a new team member, especially one you do not know, the best way to evaluate them is by assessing their past actions. Facts cannot be influenced by your intuition or a candidate's charisma.

Your company may have a formalized process with specific questions aimed to elicit responses that your company believes will deliver the best possible fit for its mission, purpose, or customer base. If this is the case, embrace this approach! Structured interviews have been demonstrated to be effective in identifying candidates with the best potential to be strong employees. If you don't have that guide, you can use the following section to develop your own set of assessment questions or perhaps add to your company's list as appropriate. Using a consistent set of questions lessens the risk of bias and leads to better choices.

If you are interviewing for entry-level positions, your candidates may not have enough experience to provide you with good examples for behavioral-based questions. I suspect that someday we'll all be using virtual reality to observe candidates facing situations, and avoid using questions altogether. In the meantime, you could turn any of these questions into hypothetical situations and still get a good idea of a candidate's thought process and values.

Here is my favorite set of questions arranged by competency. Note that each of the competency topics include a few questions along with potential positive and negative aspects of the answers you receive. It is fine to add topics based on your own business needs. If you are hiring for technical roles, you'll surely want to understand a candidate's competency in that area. If you're hiring for a management role, you'll likely include questions on motivating others and goal setting. This list of topics is basic, but critical to help you hire any great team member in any role. The topics include:

- Drive for Results
- Managing Conflict / Working with Others
- Integrity
- Diligence
- Service
- Openness to Learning

Drive for Results

Great teams are made up of members who take every opportunity to go the proverbial "extra mile" for their customers, team members, their assigned projects, and their organization. Below are a few of my favorite questions that provide insight into this essential characteristic.

- Can you give me an example of how you handled completing an assigned task when you realized it couldn't be finished during your normal working hours? What was it? What did you do?
- Can you give me an example of a creative solution you used to meet a goal from your boss or a request from a customer?
- Have you ever missed meeting an assigned goal? What was the cause? What did you do about it?
- If you think about your accomplishments at your last job, what was your proudest accomplishment? Why?
- What was the toughest job you've ever done? What made it difficult? How did you deal with that adversity?

Assessing the Answers

Positive

Clearly, a positive sign would be a candidate who says they did what was necessary to complete a task they'd promised to complete. Listen carefully for a positive "can do" attitude and creative approaches used to arrive at the best solution. Did the candidate "stick to it" through a difficult situation? Was the execution done in a spirit of partnership with their team members and especially in partnership with their boss? If so, this is an exceedingly positive sign.

Negative

On the other hand, if the candidate sounds victimized by the extra work or effort and was not energized by the opportunity to find creative solutions, this is an exceedingly bad sign. Worse yet, if the candidate cannot recall ever being called on to go beyond their normal routine to find creative solutions, then it's unlikely they'd be a good team member choice. A candidate with this profile will not only fail to deliver results but will create extra work for your existing team.

Managing Conflict / Working With Others

You can't be the Best Boss for your team if your team is in constant conflict. All workplaces have conflict; keeping that conflict productive (i.e., focused on the business versus personal issues) will keep your results strong. A team member who can't work with others will not only make your team miserable, they will negatively impact your results since everyone will spend valuable time dealing with the drama. Likewise, a team member who works well with others increases collaboration and delivers better ideas and better results. Here are a few good questions to find a candidate who will make your team happy and productive:

- Who do you like working with in your current job? Is there someone you find challenging to work with? Why?
- Give me an example of a disagreement you had with a co-worker and how you resolved it.
- Have you ever gone above and beyond to help a peer? What was the situation?

Assessing the Answers

Positive

Positive skill in this area includes the ability to address conflict quickly, with good humor and openness. Addressing a misunderstanding immediately with a co-worker is a great indication of strength and integrity. We all prefer to work with certain people, and hearing a candidate voice this and the reasons for this choice provides good insight into a potential employee.

For example, the answer might be something like this: "I'm extroverted, so I like to talk while I work. One of my co-workers is very introverted, and I've learned to tone down my commentary and allow him the quiet he needs. Since I've adjusted, we've had a great working relationship, and he now brings me problems that he thinks I will be able to help resolve." This answer indicates respect, and a willingness to adapt to peers in a way that will serve the business.

Negative

Sometimes a candidate will claim to have never experienced conflict at work. If this is the case, be very cautious! Anyone who says they haven't experienced conflict at work is either not being truthful or works very hard to avoid conflict all together (not really a positive attribute in the workplace). Such conflict-avoiding candidates may need you to resolve all conflicts, or worse, exhibit destructive passive-aggressive behaviors.

Some conflict always happens in a team. You need your employees to address differences and problems directly and respectfully with each other to create a high-performance team. Team members who don't address conflicts directly are often the same ones who create a toxic environment by being disloyal to absent team members or aligning team members against each other.

Integrity

Team members with integrity help build an environment of trust and may even provide legal protection for you and your team members. For example, if an employee believes that a product your company sells has a defect causing a safety issue, employees with integrity will likely voice that opinion. On the management side, if a problem exists within the team that you should know about, team members with integrity will let you know. Of course, this is a difficult trait to identify in an interview. Here are a few good questions that will help you identify candidates with terrific integrity:

- Give me an example of when you felt compelled to tell your boss that something was wrong. What did you say and do?
- What would you do if you saw a co-worker break the rules? Can you give me an example when this happened and what you did?
- Tell me about a mistake you made at work; what was it? What did you do once you realized you had made this mistake?

Assessing the Answers

Positive

The best candidate will be the one with the courage to speak up, even when it might be personally risky. These candidates will help you win and keep your team on track ethically. Are they willing to tell the boss the truth, even when it hurts? Employees who give you honest feedback make you a better boss and leader. Here's where you find them! If the candidate observed unethical behaviors, did they speak up, or ignore it? If they made a mistake, did they own up to the mistake immediately and inform their boss? The right answer here is a good indicator that the candidate highly values integrity and will make ethical decisions.

Negative

A lack of integrity, no matter how small, is a deal breaker! I've had to separate employees from my team for many reasons. The ethical violations have always been the most dangerous and costly. I've worked with employees who shamelessly stole, lied, harassed, and cheated. In most cases, it is hard to detect this behavior until serious harm has occurred. Any sign of evasiveness, or if they admit to staying silent in the face of unethical behavior, is a danger sign. If you detect these tendencies, continue to ask "why" until you have good evidence of a core alignment with integrity.

Diligence

You need your team to deliver results and great execution requires diligence. An employee with diligence makes your job easier since you'll have to follow up less with a self-motivated employee. Your team will appreciate a peer they can count on to deliver. Here are a few good questions to ask in order to find that candidate:

- Give me an example of a time when you felt compelled to work overtime to get the job done.
- What's the toughest job you've ever done?
- Give me an example of how you've impressed your boss with your work ethic. What was the job? What did you do that was remarkable?
- How many days last month were you late for work? (You would be shocked at how many people answer this question truthfully!)

<u>Assessing the Answers</u>

Positive
Grit! Determination! Does the example inspire you and "wow" you with the candidate's energy? You're looking for answers that indicate a willingness to work hard; a great example

would be one that demonstrates experience and comfort with difficult or challenging work. You're also looking for someone who meets your expectations on attendance and timeliness.

Negative

Energy and tenacity are core requirements for a successful team. Many skills can be trained, but training won't help someone be driven or determined to succeed. Hire for this skill and train the rest. Danger signs are answers that don't align with attendance expectations or showing up to work on time. Different definitions of "tough" assignments are also a warning sign. For example, if you were hiring a salesperson and the candidate said it was "tough" dealing with customers all day, that would indicate a candidate who was not a good fit for the job.

Service

Whether you're hiring some to work with external or internal customers, a real commitment to service is a key competency. Yes, dealing with customers of any kind can be difficult, but those who fill these roles must LOVE their customers. Here are a few questions to find employees who are passionate about service:

- When have you "broken the rules" for a customer?
- Tell me about a difficult customer you dealt with. What happened?
- Give me an example of a customer compliment you've received. What was it? Why did that customer appreciate your solution?

- Tell me about your favorite customer. What makes them special?

<u>Assessing the Answers</u>

Positive

Did the candidate exhibit self-control? Did they turn the situation around? Did they use humor (appropriately) to defuse the situation? Do they look for solutions or just fall back on the rules? You're looking for positive emotions that are elicited when the candidate thinks about customers. The best service people I've hired physically "light up" when they talk about customers or their teams. That's the enthusiasm that creates a terrific service experience.

Negative

If you sense anger in the interviewee, it's likely your candidate can't keep their cool, and this is not a candidate committed to service. Likewise, any complaints about demanding customers (internal or external) deserve deeper investigation to ensure your candidate truly values service.

Openness to Learning

The best bosses celebrate improvement and growth for everyone on their team. Growth indicates a willingness to change and that is the most important skill in today's constantly changing business environment.

Here are a few questions to help you find these employees:

- What do your peers (or boss) like about working with you? What would they change?
- What are your strengths? What do you need to work on to improve? What have you done to address those needs?
- Tell me about a change (new policy or change to process, for example) that occurred at work. What was it? What did you think about the change? How did you deal with that change?
- Tell me about a mistake you made at work. What did you learn?

Assessing the Answers

Positive

We ALL have things that we can improve! A candidate with a "growth mindset" will realize this and is comfortable with acknowledging both their weaknesses and strengths. You are looking for answers that indicate the candidate is willing to embrace change and views new processes or policies as opportunities for learning.

Negative

Most of us hate having to answer the interview question about our weaknesses. We think that this question is a trap designed to disqualify us. That's not the point; openness, honesty, and transparency are the real purpose. If a candidate has no idea what people think of them, or won't admit to any weaknesses, they are unlikely to take any feedback in a way that will help them to grow. The candidate's weakness is unimportant (unless the weakness is integrity!); what you'd like to see is that your candidate has self-awareness and sees mistakes as a necessary part of learning and growth.

Analysis

Whatever your questions, you're looking for a better understanding of your candidate. Think about these three areas:

1. What did they do?
2. Why and how did they do it?
3. How would that apply in the role you're hiring for?

Team Input

Most hiring decisions come after several rounds of interviews, including a round involving your team. One leader I know decided to audit all the hires her team had made that didn't work out. What she found was that in each case, one person on the team voted "no" and was overruled. She instituted a rule that the team must respect one another's views in hiring and only hire candidates who receive unanimous support. This one change significantly improved the leader's hiring success rate.

Each interviewer brings unique insights about a job candidate. Multiple interviews ensure a clear and accurate picture of a candidate. You can accomplish this by assigning each interviewer one question from the competencies we've noted thus far in this chapter. Doing so will provide multiple perspectives on each competency while also eliminating the possibility that your candidate will get bored answering the same questions again and again.

Exercise – Developing an Interview Guide

Creating high-performance teams requires including members with many different styles and experiences. Shared values are critical to success. If your company values integrity, then you would likely avoid hiring someone focused on winning at all costs. Nor would you hire someone willing to undermine their peers for their own benefit, if your organization values collaboration.

Think back to the earlier discussion on defining core values. Here's a list of these key values as a reminder for this exercise:

- *Respect*
- *Teamwork*
- *Innovation*
- *Integrity*
- *Self-Control*
- *Service*
- *Collaboration*
- *Trustworthiness*

No matter where you work, these are likely core organizational values. Companies focus on hiring employees with these values because they cannot be taught, unlike skills. That's why it's important to ask questions that will reveal if these fundamental values are shared by a potential employee.

Exercise:

This exercise will help you craft questions that will give insight into an interviewee's alignment with these values. Develop your personal set of favorite interview questions. Use your company values, the key values we've listed above, and the key competencies discussed earlier as the basis for this work. For each value or competency, choose your own questions, either from those questions I've given you, or questions of your own design.

The questions that you create should allow you to assess the three hiring points we covered earlier:

1. What did the candidate do before?
2. Why and how did they do it?
3. How would this past experience apply in the role you're hiring for?

As you craft your questions, ask yourself: What would this value look like in practice? What behaviors demonstrate this value? What behaviors would violate these values? Use your own experiences as you craft these questions. Here's an example to help you:

Value / Competency: Loyalty to the Absent

Description of skilled behavior: Addresses conflict directly with the person involved, avoids gossip, speaks positively of peers to co-workers.

Interview Question: Tell me about a time that someone shared negative information with you about a peer. What did you do?

Your personal favorite interview questions:

1. Value / Competency:
Description of skilled behavior:

_____

Interview Question:

_____

2. Value / Competency:
Description of skilled behavior:

_____

Interview Question:

_____

3. Value / Competency:
Description of skilled behavior:

_____

Interview Question:

_____

4. Value / Competency:
Description of skilled behavior:

_____

Interview Question:

_____

Step 3 – Choosing the Best Candidate

If you've carefully chosen your candidates, asked the right questions, and analyzed the answers correctly, choosing the best candidate should be the least difficult step. Even if you have several candidates that you believe are perfect fits for your team, making a final choice is a combination of logic, empirical evidence, and your judgment. The process I recommend involves the use of a question set based on the six competencies discussed above: drive for results, managing conflict/working with others, integrity, diligence, service, and openness to learning, as well as any additional areas you think are important.

Research has shown that scoring interviews leads to more accurate and less biased assessments. I would recommend you rate each candidate on a scale of 1-5:

1: Poorly aligned with expectations for this area.
2: Below expectations for this area.
3: Meets the expectations for this area.
4: Exceeds the expectations for this area.
5: Wow!

Clearly, using a rating system is somewhat subjective, but the scores will give you a simple tool to compare the candidates to one another and help you identify strengths and weaknesses easily. This methodology also helps you to effectively compare candidates even if they've been interviewed hours or days apart. Such time gaps often make it difficult to equitably compare candidates that you interviewed two weeks ago, with those you interviewed more recently; i.e., you are more favorably inclined to more recent interviewees.

Here's an example of how this system is applied to a set of candidates across six key competency indicators:

Candidate:	Experience Match:	Q1: Drive for Results	Q2: Conflict	Q3: Integrity	Q4: Diligence	Q5: Service	Q6: Open to Learn	Total Average Score:
Javier	5	4	3	4	3	5	4	4.00
Sammy	3	3	2	5	5	4	5	3.86
Jennifer	4	2	2	4	3	3	2	2.86
Cedric	3	4	3	5	4	4	4	3.86
Amanda	5	4	5	1	4	5	4	4.00

When reviewing these sample results in Figure 3.2, some clear indicators emerge. First, you can quickly eliminate the bottom scoring candidates. At the top of the scale are Javier and Amanda with equal scores. But note that Amanda's integrity score indicates she is well below expectations. In this case, Javier is the smart choice given the importance placed on integrity for your team's health. If the choice isn't this clear-cut, you might have to make your choice based on your judgment, or perhaps rely on a reference check to help you decide.

This scoring methodology is particularly helpful if you are using multiple interviewers. Scoring will move the conversation and decision making toward the facts and examples that led to the ratings and away from emotion ("I just really liked him!"). While this approach takes some time and effort, the payoff is a hire that will benefit your team and your results.

Contacting References

You can learn a lot about a candidate from the interview process described above. But here's the rub—in all my years of interviewing, no candidate who turned out to be dishonest ever told me that they believed in stealing or cheating or unethical behavior. Some candidates told me they were terrific team players but behaved in a completely opposite way once they were on the job. I find candidate-provided references can sometimes be a waste of time; if I wanted to hear only your wonderful traits, I could just call your mom directly.

However, I do encourage you to check references on every candidate. Choosing to add someone to your team is the most important decision you will make; any information that will help you make a better decision is extremely valuable.

For example, I was once interviewing a management candidate who had been vetted through seven interviews and an external recruiter. Something about the candidate seemed "off" to me, even though he had the perfect answers to my questions. I checked a reference at the candidate's prior company and found out that not only had the candidate lied about his position, but he had also been fired for sexual harassment!

That reference saved me from giving my team a peer who would have violated values of integrity, and certainly created a massive problem for me. Contacting references is a final check on your decision and allows you to build your network with other leaders. This is a great opportunity to learn more about your candidate; taking the time for references is an investment that will pay off with a deeper understanding of your candidate and a better decision for your team.

Of course, you should always be developing your internal talent bench. You owe it to your team to look to them first for opportunities. Developing your team for promotion creates terrific loyalty and commitment. And once you have built a high-performance team, you'll find your people promoted throughout the company. What an awesome legacy!

Learn from the Best: Advice from Great Leaders
Being a great boss requires commitment not only to your team, but also to your personal growth. Listening to successful leaders accelerates our success by allowing us to learn from their

experiences. I've asked the same questions in each of these interviews to demonstrate the many paths to great leadership.

Dave Burwick, Former CEO, Peet's Coffee & Tea

Peet's Coffee is the premier specialty coffee and tea company in the United States. Under Dave's leadership, Peet's has expanded to more than double annual sales and store locations. Prior to Peet's, Dave previously served as the president of Weight Watchers North America, and the CMO of PepsiCo Americas, among other roles. Dave holds an MBA from Harvard Business School and is well known for his commitment to his people and his team.

What quality do you think is critical to be a great boss?

Empathy is so important. You need to understand the people you work with to understand what motivates them to reach their potential. If you're not a good listener, or ego-driven, you're not going to see it. You will be successful if you serve your team well.

What mistakes do you see new leaders make?

Leaders often fail by trying to do their old job. When you transition to a new and bigger role, you need to consciously change your mindset, to readjust priorities and think about how you're going to lead differently. You've been successful in your prior role and are habitual in your approach; now you need to think more broadly. Becoming more self-aware and understanding what you're about will help you create authenticity, and people will be much more likely to follow you.

If you had advice for yourself in your first management role, what would it be?

Use this opportunity to reinvent yourself and to address your opportunities. A big transition for me was moving from the role of CMO for Pepsi in Canada to the President job. I found that the group expected me to represent the marketing perspective, which I had done for fifteen years. Once I let go of my old role, I became a more mature leader and better served my team.

What do you think makes a boss great?

A great boss knows you personally and professionally. They understand what motivates you and give you regular constructive feedback to make you better. A great boss gives you the freedom to grow and lead. You must be humble enough to know that you can't do it on your own and encourage your team to share their ideas.

Do you have any secrets for building a great team?

I believe in the Medici effect. People who are very different in background, skills, race, or gender, for example, get the best results. You may not gravitate to people who are unlike you immediately, but hiring people who are different will bring you better results than hiring clones. Honesty and transparency in a team are critical for success. Establishing trust quickly with a new team by demonstrating that you're looking out for their interests and are supportive of them will lead to collaboration and speed.

How do you stay healthy while doing this job?

Good lifestyle happens when it's automatic—you really have to schedule workouts and good habits. Being present when you go home is so important. You may not have as many hours with those you care about as you'd like, so be fully present when you are together. The quality of your time together is more important than the quantity.

What advice do you have to address employee performance issues?

Be honest, transparent, and timely. When people are not performing, they know it. The first step is to tell them the truth about their performance and give them a chance to improve. Leaders often let things languish, and delay doesn't help. You've invested in this person, and you owe them the chance to improve.

Do you have a favorite interview question that helps you hire great people?

Understanding the formative experiences that made you who you are is very informative. Judging for cultural fit is both instinctive and intuitive; it is more about capability than about talent. When you hire people, you're making a bet on them, so make a good one!

What's Next

We've covered the critical importance of hiring to your success and the success of your team. In the next chapter, I'll show you how to find great people with recruiting strategies that work. You'll learn how to build a high-performance team and plan proactively to prevent "Talent Fires" with an ever-ready pipeline of talent.

Chapter 4

DELIVER EXCEPTIONAL RESULTS

IN THIS CHAPTER:
- *Setting Goals: Theory and Practice*
- *Managing Performance for Exceptional Results*
- *Consistency Equals Engagement*
- *Rewards and Recognition*
- *Learn from the Best*

The best leaders work hard to create conditions that allow every employee to succeed. This essential help begins by setting clear expectations. One of the most common mistakes first-time managers or team leaders make is providing too little specific instruction when they assign a task. Sometimes important task details are simply glossed over to save time or because the person assigning the task thinks the details are obvious. Sometimes leaders (especially inexperienced ones) don't provide enough detailed instructions because they are not comfortable in the role of "boss."

Unfortunately, these and other task communication mistakes have consequences on two levels. On one level, poor instruction creates frustration and disappointment among other team members who are asked to do the task again; in addition, team members charged with repeating the task are likely to resent their boss's failure to provide clear instructions in the first place. On another perhaps more visible level, the financial consequences to your company of paying twice for the same work cannot be ignored.

Most organizations spend a significant amount of resources to ensure their employees have clearly defined broad goals and performance expectations. Still, it falls to team managers and leaders to make sure employees meet these expectations in ways that allow them to be successful. This chapter describes some methods and practices that will help you do this important job; but remember, this is certainly not a full catalog. Instead, what follows are important, top-line considerations designed to help new managers set and then explain the execution of specific goals in ways that make you the Best Boss possible.

> *"Because a thing seems difficult for you, do not think it impossible for anyone to accomplish."*
> — *Marcus Aurelius*

About Setting Goals

One of the biggest problems you're likely to face as a new manager or team leader is that setting goals and expectations (especially when specific goal metrics are included) can be an intimidating process for many people. It would be great if every employee reacted with enthusiasm to measurable performance challenges, but the first thought for many employees is "What happens if I don't meet that goal?" As a leader, your challenge is to help those you manage get beyond this tendency to focus on the downside (failure), and not the upside (success).

Despite the worry that many employees experience, setting challenging goals drives better and more satisfying results for your team. In their seminal book on goal setting, Dr. Edwin Locke and Dr. Gary Latham demonstrated that people perform better (not worse, as you might expect) when given difficult goals rather than easily attainable ones. (10)

While this may seem counter-intuitive, it turns out that challenging goals trigger our attention and our energy. The fact is, when given hard challenges we tend to respond with surprising results. In reviewing numerous studies conducted over a decade, Locke and Latham found that specific and challenging goals led to higher performance. Vague conditional instructions such as "just do your best" did nothing to ease employee worry or increase goal attainment. The key to exceptional results is challenge! The bottom line is that challenging goals focuses employees' attention toward action and increases both motivation and persistence. (11)

I have seen challenging goals pay off with unprecedented results time and again during my career. I consciously pushed myself to set goals for my team that were uncomfortable and caused even me to question their aggressiveness; i.e., I was secretly questioning whether I was setting my team up to fail. However, my team consistently out-performed my expectations and delivered results that surprised (and delighted) our organization.

How do you know if a goal is challenging enough? You should always strive for improvement by setting ever-higher standards. In fact, a good sign is a slight feeling of nervousness about achieving the goals you've set. Another good sign that you're on the right track is the number of detractors who complain that your goals are too aggressive. However, don't take too rigid a stance. If everyone on your team questions a goal and offers legitimate concerns, you might have set your benchmark too high. In time, your insight and intuition will tell you when you've reached this important tipping point.

The bottom line is that setting easily achievable goals is tempting—especially if your performance is judged by your team's success—but building an outstanding team requires setting challenging and specific goals!

Could you just tell me what you want?

Have you ever worked for a boss who was unclear about what they wanted? Early in my career I was working in a department store, and my boss asked me to put up a new summer clothing display. I didn't have any idea how to rock a visual display—I was a political science major in college. I figured I would give it my best shot and spent a few hours creating a display of shorts and tees that I thought would delight our customers. When I unveiled my masterpiece for my boss, she hated it. She shared the ways I had violated visual design principles (who knew you shouldn't display shorts higher on the wall than tees?) and directed me to re-do the display. Clearly, this was a waste of money since my employer had to pay me twice for a single, simple task. Specificity is critically important, especially with new employees.

Setting Goals and Managing Performance

Even if you know your team members consistently thrive on meeting challenging goals, you're still likely to hear objections from at least one person on even the most engaged teams. This section provides specific tips and techniques that will help you set reasonable expectations, assist your team in achieving them, and finally, celebrate success on completion.

Handling Objections

Leaders must be comfortable facing pushback from their team members on many fronts, including company-wide policy or practice changes. Pushback on your individual employee goal setting responsibility is an expected part of the job. As such, you can expect to hear objections to any new or higher performance standard, but you cannot let the skeptics dominate. In most cases, an open discussion about the change among team members usually will get most on board. But if you need further evidence that the goal is reasonable, you might try pointing to a star performer who has already met the higher goal or standard. After all, it's hard to say achieving a goal is impossible when you have direct evidence. Our belief about our ability to achieve significantly impacts our results. Seeing someone else accomplish a goal we once thought impossible sparks our thinking and our belief about what is possible. Success breeds success.

So, what should a great boss keep in mind when they work with team members to establish reasonable performance goals? It's a complex task, but you can make it simple by focusing on these key areas:

- Set Challenging, Measurable Goals
- Identify Risks and Unintended Consequences
- Regularly Check Progress
- Judge Results Equitably
- Reward and Recognize Results

Set Challenging and Measurable Goals

Leaders don't get respect for making goals complicated, numerous, or hard to understand. In fact, the effect is just the opposite and results in poor performance. Getting great results from your team requires you to make choices and prioritize. If a goal or task is complex, break it down into manageable chunks.

For example, consider what parts of the goal might be done now and what parts later in the month or quarter. Dividing a very complex goal ensures focus and increases the likelihood your team will achieve its goals. Once you have these milestone goals identified, assign deadlines. Setting clear timelines for goals provides clarity for your team and gives your team agreed upon performance expectation benchmarks. Without milestones, you might reach the end of a project or reporting period and discover you've left out an important project task or activity. In addition to tracking progress, milestones provide early opportunities for recognition or coaching that will keep your team engaged and on track.

Goals should be extremely clear and measurable. Answering the question, "Did I achieve this goal?" should be easy to answer for any team member. Without this clarity, it's likely your team members will accomplish the wrong goal or inadequately achieve the right goal. That's why details need to be spelled out or at least acknowledged during the goal setting process, even if you think they are obvious details and clarifications.

A very expensive example of providing specific details when assigning tasks (and making sure the details you provide are correct) happened in 2014 when France's state-controlled railway operator SNCF spent $20.5 billion on new trains that were too wide for many of the country's station platforms. The mistake cost the government $68.4 million, which was the cost of widening the stations that were too narrow for the new train. As it turned out, when the manufacturer asked for the train station dimensions, SNCF provided all the station dimensions for those built in the past thirty years. Unfortunately, there were many stations in the country's south and west regions that were fifty years old or more, and these were not included in the list of stations. (12) Details matter, and missing those details can cost you millions!

Exercise – Clear Direction

Giving your team members clear directions begins with understanding your own definition of high expectations. If your organization provides metrics you can use (number of sales, time required to do a specific task), that's great. But you still should have your own standard that defines a high performing employee. Answer the following questions before moving on to the next section.

- What does great or exceptional performance mean to you? For example, is it doing more than was required or just meeting the goals you or your organization have set?

- What behaviors do you associate with high performing employees? For example, engagement, enthusiasm, or collaboration. How important are any such behaviors to your definition of success?
- What are your expectations about communication? Do you want to know about any obstacles your employee encounters, or would you like them to first try to resolve on their own? When should your employee communicate with you on progress toward their goal?
- What are your company's goals for the year, month, or week? What is your role in delivering these goals?
- What are your personal goals for the year, month, or week? Are they clear, challenging, and measurable?
- What are your goals for your employees for the year, month, or week? Are they clear, challenging, and measurable?

Identify Risk and Unintended Consequences

Goal setting creates energy and action toward achievement and results, but it may also result in unintended consequences. You can avoid these consequences with sensible planning. Let me give you an example from my own experience.

I had a goal to increase checkout speed at a large retail store as part of an initiative to increase customer satisfaction. In response, my team developed a plan to accurately capture metrics on how long it took each cashier to process a customer at their station. On the face of it, it sounded like a reasonable approach, but here's what happened:

Using the collected data, we devised new ways to process our customer's orders that would speed up the processing time tremendously. However, the faster checkout times did not improve our customer satisfaction survey data. Puzzled, I spent some time observing how cashiers applied the new checkout protocols. What I found at the checkout stations was an ingenious solution the cashiers created to "game" the new process. Instead of folding items and removing the security tags from each item as it was scanned, the cashiers did this time-consuming work before scanning the first item. Timing metrics were based on how much time elapsed between when the first item was scanned, and last item was scanned and totaled, so this prepping allowed the cashier to take longer with the trans-action, without that time reflected in the reporting. Cashiers appeared to be faster on our reporting (thus pleasing their bosses) but checking out was actually slower for customers.

With this new, accurate timing information, we adapted both our reporting method and the directions given to the cashiers. These changes improved the speed of checkout as originally intended and achieved the goal of a faster checkout for customers.

Wells Fargo Bank offers another spectacular example of not considering unintended consequences when it set aggressive goals for credit card sign-ups for its front-line bank employees. (13) While sales goals were met, the methods were fraudulent, and more than two million customers were impacted. Not only was this policy damaging to the bank's reputation, Wells Fargo also eventually paid $185 million in fines. More than five thou-sand employees lost their jobs as well. Certainly, this was not the work of a great boss!

Leaders can avoid the risk of unintended consequences by clearly identifying risks before goals are communicated to teams. Identify (or imagine) a challenging, important goal for your team. Now, take a moment to complete the following exercise to identify unintended consequences and potential mitigation steps:

Potential unintended consequences:

- How could an employee "cheat" to achieve this goal?
- If an employee re-directed all their attention to this goal, what other areas of the business would suffer?
- Is the timeline realistic to achieve this goal?
- Could this goal incentivize employees to withhold support or collaboration with their peers to achieve this goal? (Is achieving the goal contingent on doing better than a peer?)

Plan to address risk:

- Identify observation or reporting that would identify any unethical behavior. (For example, Wells Fargo could have reviewed customer account information with customers to identify fraud.)
- Adjust any timelines that are so tight that they make goal achievement impossible without cheating.
- Adjust the number of goals and expectations to make sure they are achievable on their own and taken together are not overwhelming.
- Adjust your goal setting to avoid any peer-to-peer competition. (For example, avoid a goal that rewards performance over the group average, but instead rewards performance over previous performance. Ranking

individuals against each other will lead to negative team behavior and generally leads to lower results overall.)

Planning will protect you and your team from unethical behavior or unintended consequences and allow you to deliver performance with challenging goals. Now, let's move on to your role in reviewing progress.

Regularly Check Progress

Consistent feedback helps ensure that employees are on track to meet the measures you've set. In this regard, leaders also serve as a coach and in some ways, are a success cheerleader for team members. It's your job to guide team members towards delivering great results. This is not achieved by telling those you manage what to do and how to do it, but by helping them find their own path to solutions. Coaching is a bit of a leadership tightrope; you likely do have terrific ideas (you are the boss, after all), but the trick is to know when to gently advise and when to hold back advice.

Providing honest, straightforward feedback is critical to the success of your employees. While both managers and employees dread critical feedback, it is the only way to improve performance. The courage to give feedback, especially when it is not positive, strengthens the contribution you make to your employee's success and ultimately your company's success. The Best Boss helps their employees grow and succeed in a supportive way. Balance negative feedback with frequent acknowledgement of what an employee is doing right. You'll find tips on authentic recognition later in this chapter.

Successful Progress Meetings

Because each person who works on your team is unique, there is no perfect formula to give employee feedback that will produce the best results, but here is one example of how to have a successful progress meeting. Depending on your time and resources or established company policy, you should sit down with your team members at regular intervals to compare their progress against goals (once a week, every two weeks, monthly). The meeting should cover these essential questions:

1. What is going well (or what is working)? Why?
2. What is not going (or working) so well? Why?
3. What actions can you take to stay on track or get back on track?
4. What support does your employee need from you to succeed? (Training, resources, or money for instance.)
5. How can you help the employee stick to their commitment? (For example, you could use a measurement of progress, or schedule an update meeting.)

Here's an example of how such a conversation might proceed:

- **Employee:** Hey, I fixed that report on monthly sales. I'm sorry it was wrong the first time.
- **Best Boss:** I'm glad you fixed it. What caused the error?
- **Employee:** I was just rushing to get through all my work, and I didn't check the data. I feel stupid, but there is just so much to do here!
- **Best Boss:** I hear you, there is a lot on your plate.

- **Employee:** Of course, it took me longer because I made the error. I really don't have time to do things twice.
- **Best Boss:** Agreed! Could you commit to double checking before you turn in reports to save this aggravation? What about having your peer look over the big reports to catch any errors you might have missed?
- **Employee:** Yeah, I think that would make a difference. I know how to do this, I just need to be more careful.
- **Best Boss:** On a scale of one to ten, how motivated are you to follow through on that commitment?
- **Employee:** Probably an eight.
- **Best Boss:** Why didn't you pick a lower number? (Asking this question helps employees to articulate their own motivation, solidifying their own commitment.)
- **Employee:** Because I want to do great work here, and I don't want to waste my time or yours.
- **Best Boss:** Terrific! Let's meet again in two weeks, and see if this approach works.

You can see that this approach takes critical thinking, and TIME! It is so much easier to just tell an associate, "Hey, you screwed up that report... Fix it!" However, the time you invest in this conversation will lead to better long-term results for you, your employee, and your company.

Judge Results Equitably

Your team is counting on you to provide a fair playing field. Since business priorities sometimes change swiftly, it is tempting to just adjust goals to match the business need of the moment. Yes, your boss may identify a new opportunity, or your competition may develop a new solution that requires action to protect your business. However, changing the "goal post" is frustrating for team members, so if possible, you should avoid changing goals without careful consideration. Generally, you have three options to deal with these business environment changes:

1. Wait and add the goal to the next review cycle.
2. Address the business need without creating a goal. This gives you time to resolve the issue and begin to change focus for your team while still preserving the integrity of your direction and goals.
3. Adjust the goal to address the opportunity and discuss the change with your team. Note that changing goals may result in your team losing trust and confidence in your leadership. Moreover, your team may hold back their effort as they wait for the next change in direction. Members will also be extremely frustrated and be less willing to give more effort than their job requires.

One way to keep consistent goals in a quickly changing business is to set goals for your team quarterly instead of annually. This approach allows you to adapt, be competitive, and still maintain your team's trust in your direction.

In the end, you don't want to surprise your team members. Think about your goal planning as an open book test: you want everyone to pass with flying colors.

Consistency Equals Engagement

One of the side benefits of consistent goal setting is team member engagement. Challenging goals create meaningful work, which creates engaged employees. It's an extremely important outcome. Especially when you consider recent Gallup research that revealed engaged employees outperform in key business measures including: customer metrics, profitability, employee turnover, absenteeism, safety, and productivity. (14) These benefits dovetail nicely with the other leadership behaviors that encourage engagement already noted in this book, including having a service attitude and focusing on values.

Recognition!

Most of us are motivated by a sincere recognition of our work; a "thank you" goes much farther than you realize. In fact, the consulting firm McKinsey (15) found that praise from managers is the number one performance motivator, more than even financial incentives. You'll experience better results if you appreciate your team. In an independent survey of employees, Globoforce found that 78 percent of workers said that they would work harder if their efforts were better recognized and appreciated. (16) If you miss the opportunity to recognize your team, you're missing the opportunity to deliver outstanding results!

One of the benefits of a values-focused leadership approach is that you have a clear notion of a team member's core values. This information allows you to provide high performing employees with an appropriate and appreciated reward. This recognition approach truly increases engagement. If your team members feel appreciated, they are far more likely to give all their talents to accomplishing both your goals and those of the organization.

How to Say Thank You

Here are a few ways to say *Thank you!* to your team members.

- **An actual, written note**. I recently asked some leaders if they have ever received a hand-written "thank you" from a boss. Their answers reminded me of the power of sincere, written appreciation. One manager told me, "The fact that the note was hand written really took the recognition to another level. Instead of a simple email or a phone call, this person took time out of their day to write me. When I received these notes, I displayed them with pride in my office and they meant so much more to me than the sender realized." Don't you want to make people feel like that?

- **Be spontaneous**. Years ago, I received a phone call out of the blue from the chairman of our company to thank me for some particularly important business results. I still remember it to this day. When someone who works for you does something you appreciate, waste no time in saying thank you; the element of surprise helps to emphasize the feeling attached to your appreciation.

- **Encourage peer recognition**. A joint survey conducted by the Society of Human Resource Managers and Globoforce found that recognition programs that include peer appreciation are 35.7 percent more likely to have a positive impact on financial results as compared to manager-only recognition. (17) Peer recognition is also a sure path to trust and co-operation within your team. You can lead your team to overcome very human competition conflicts by allowing the team members to appreciate each other. A great practice is to begin all your meetings with recognition. Just make sure to remind the team ahead of your meetings to ensure members are prepared with meaningful and sincere appreciation.

- **Get your boss to say thanks.** Ask your boss to recognize someone on your team; it gives your employee visibility, confidence, and opportunity. This can be as natural as, "Maria just completed that complicated transfer; would you mention it to her the next time you see her?" Bonus: makes your boss look good, too.

Finally, make recognition sincere. You may feel you're giving too much recognition, but I'll tell you, that's nearly impossible. If you want a behavior to continue, you need to recognize the behavior whether it's always being at work on time, or going beyond the expected to help customers or another team member. To use a familiar phrase in a radically different context, "If you see something, say something."

"You get what you celebrate."
—*Frank Blake, CEO, Home Depot*

Exercise – Recognition

Take a moment to plan an approach to recognizing your team. The leaders who are the best at recognition make it a priority and a habit. Developing a plan for recognition will protect this leadership activity from all the competing pressures and priorities you will face. Answer the following questions to establish your plan:

- What will be your personal recognition approach? Will you use written notes? Email? Social media?
- What results do you want to recognize consistently? Looking at your goals, how will you recognize performance against those goals? Will you recognize results weekly, monthly, or quarterly? Are there reports or metrics that would lead you to recognize results? Besides business goals, identify behaviors that reflect the team's values to recognize as well. (Remember, your recognition sends a message to your team about what is most important!)
- When will you fit recognition into your schedule? Some leaders set aside a few minutes at the end of the day, some prefer Friday afternoons as a time of reflection, planning, and recognition. Choose your time, and then block your calendar to protect your commitment to recognizing your team.

Learn from the Best: Advice from Great Leaders

Being a great boss requires commitment not only to your team, but also to your personal growth. Listening to successful leaders accelerates our success by allowing us to learn from their experiences. I've asked the same questions in each of these interviews to demonstrate the many paths to great leadership.

Monika Fahlbusch, Chief Employee
Experience Officer, BMC Software

Monika Fahlbusch is the Chief Employee Experience Officer at BMC Software, a company in the IT management space. BMC

Software has over six thousand employees around the world and the Experience Team has four hundred fifty people focused on employee experience. Monika has a background leading teams in both IT and HR in high tech companies for the last thirty years.

What quality do you think is critical to be a great boss?

A great boss pushes you very hard, actually. They set a simple, executable, aggressive vision. This vision is often unsettling because it's challenging; you'll find motivation and anxiety in equal measure. It's critical to give fair and honest feedback; a great boss is not soft, but open and fair. You get the sense that a great boss has your back!

What mistakes do you see new leaders make?

The biggest thing I see first time leaders and new executives struggle with is a belief that they must appear perfect. It's important to bring issues and problems to the table and share them with your boss and team. A good script is to say with confidence, "I want to give you a signal fire. I'm concerned about this, we'll watch it." It's not a weakness to identify a problem, and it drives so much credibility when leaders share honestly.

If you had advice for yourself in your first management role, what would it be?

The best advice I've received was, "You're doing a great job, and you're working hard. But if your car burst into flames in the parking lot, not a single person would grab a hose or bucket to put it out. You've got some teamwork to do." I realized that some people on my team had to go. With others, I needed to repair relationships; I was doing too much myself. I would go from a problem to an answer; I didn't take anyone with me. I learned to take people with me and gather input to get to better answers and a better team.

Do you have any secrets for building a great team?

I can visualize five people that I trust completely and that I could put in *any* job. They are smart and reflect positive values. I recommend that leaders identify people like this, lean on them, and take them with you in any way you can. When you have great people, you're in the zone—it's real high performance. Having people you trust overrides a lack of experience. It is incumbent on you to support people like this when you give them a stretch assignment. If they fail, they know it's okay, that you'll take care of them; that's where trust becomes so important. You can't teach agility. Certain people have it, and these people are golden!

How do you stay healthy doing this job?

You have to keep perspective—you're selling software or jeans. With six thousand employees, it's important to come in with optimism and balance. They can't see you stressed, or you'll impact all six thousand people. Being a curious citizen of the world creates balance and ideas. Taking care of yourself physically is important. Sharing your personal experience is important. For example, saying, "I took some calls from home so that I could visit my dad today" demonstrates your humanity, and makes these conversations safe for your team.

What advice do you have to address employee performance issues?

It never gets easier. I think it's just human nature to avoid conflict. If we can stare at the issue in the cold light of day and deal with it sooner rather than later, we'll be better off. If we're honest with ourselves, we can see the issue. Don't ever kid yourself: every member of your team knows the issue!

Do you have a favorite interview question that helps you hire great people?

The idea of an "interview" is really changing. Today, it's more about developing a relationship. I like to ask questions that have nothing to do with the job. In my role, by the time I'm interviewing you, I know you can do the job. Your ability to tell a story, relate to me, demonstrate confidence, and tell me about a time you made a mistake are most important to me.

Finally, I'll leave you with this simple truth—there's nothing like winning to inspire and motivate a team!

What's Next

You've hired a great team, defined your values, and set clear and challenging goals. How do you make sure your team lives the values that will create success? How do you create a workplace that is supportive, results-oriented, and fun? How can you help your team resolve conflicts in a manner that builds relationships and leads to better outcomes? How can you lead meetings that are never boring? Read on for the answers!

Chapter 5

CREATE A HIGH-PERFORMANCE CULTURE

IN THIS CHAPTER:
* *Basics of Building a Positive Culture*
* *What Creates Good Team Culture*
* *Effective Meetings Build Respect*
* *Handling Conflict*
* *Learn from the Best*

Everything you do as a leader impacts your team's culture. Most companies understand how this organizational dynamic can positively or negatively impact a whole range of essential hallmarks of a successful company—engagement, productivity, retention, innovation, just to name a few. Whether you lead a project team, a company division, or an entire organization, how you handle this key responsibility will ultimately determine your success.

So, how do you begin delivering on this commitment to create a positive and supportive workplace culture given the emotional and social importance of work in our lives? As previously noted, money incentives do not translate directly into employee motivation and engagement. What's important to most employees is a sense of purpose—making a positive contribution to the world—along with the emotional rewards of service to others and a strong sense of job competence. If you build a healthy team or organizational culture based on actions that support these employee needs for workplace meaning, your job as a leader will be immensely easier and ultimately much more successful.

> *"A boat doesn't go forward if each one is rowing their own way."*
> —*Swahili Proverb*

Basics of Building a Positive Culture

As you'll see, this chapter describes a variety of ways a leader can build a positive and supportive culture for employees. However, the basic rules are simple and reflect in large measure a "golden rule" approach of treating others the way you would like to be treated.

1. **Communicate Appreciation:** Make sure your team knows that you appreciate their work, and tell them how their work (both individually and collectively) contributes to the company's overall success.
2. **Communicate Impact:** Show your team how the work they do contributes to the greater good. As noted, a service approach to leadership emphasizes the connection between the work we do and its potential to positively

impact the world around us—locally, nationally, and worldwide. Although this connection might not be obvious in every case, most leaders who give this idea a little thought quickly see these connections. While making money is quite motivating, most people want to contribute to the world in a broader way, to feel that their work makes a difference. Whatever your business, finding the link to a bigger purpose will energize your team and create authentic commitment. This purpose might be providing employees the opportunity to realize upward mobility and success, spreading kindness through customer interactions, or developing life-saving drugs. Communicating the impact of your team's work on the world is a terrific way to build engagement and commitment.

You might think making a case for deeper meaning or community impact for every type of business would be difficult, but even the most profit-oriented business has the potential to make a positive difference. I once worked with a retailer that sold low-price clothing and home goods that developed a deep sense of mission and purpose among its employees by connecting their work to the positive impact stores had in the community by providing empowerment, dignity, and respect to others.

I'll never forget a young woman who had been homeless during her high school years and her story of shuttling between spending her nights in shelters, couches, and cars. She said she was grateful for our discount store because the clothes she bought there allowed her to feel like she fit in with her peers and gave her confidence that she belonged in school. The work the teams did in stores directly impacted people in very meaningful ways, and sharing these stories helped build job commitment and a sense of purpose for employees that led to terrific results for customers, the company, and for employees.

3. **Encourage Collaboration:** Encourage your team to collaborate and share information freely and to celebrate and reward their successes collectively. In many ways, this behavior forms the bedrock of a strong team or organizational culture. Unfortunately, not every leader is able to follow this pathway. Leaders who feel a need to "be in charge" of their employees might find this approach difficult if not impossible to follow. Leaders who use a servant leadership approach will find the approach a more natural fit—with the following caveat: Being a servant leader doesn't mean you're a pushover. Sometimes you need to deliver tough messages, but if you focus on making the employee better and use the confrontation to enable their success, your message won't be heard as demoralizing criticism. Even if you must "let an employee go" your honest expressed desire for the employee's success will reduce typical reactions of anger and defensiveness.

What Creates Good Team Culture

Creating a productive team culture is worth a book on its own, but fortunately, Google recently provided some guidance to help us answer this question (what can't Google answer?!). Google's team project was titled "Aristotle," (18) and the company marshaled a group of world-class researchers to figure out the key factors that create a high-performance team. Surprisingly, the research found that *who* was on a team (for example, introverts, extroverts, friends, or strangers) made little difference to team performance; *how* the team worked together was found to be the most critical factor. The study was focused on Google's teams, but the lessons learned are relevant for any team's success. Here are the defining values they discovered for high-performance teams and questions to help you assess your own team:

1. **Psychological safety:** Can we take risks without feeling insecure or embarrassed?
2. **Dependability:** Can we count on each other to do high quality work on time?
3. **Structure and clarity:** Are goals, roles, and execution plans on our team clear?
4. **Meaning of work:** Are we working on something that is personally important for each of us?
5. **Impact of work:** Do we fundamentally believe that the work we're doing matters? (19)

Clearly, these are positive characteristics that would help any team be successful. But how do you build such a strong team if you're the leader charged with this responsibility? The first point to remember is you oversee the culture; i.e., how you behave and what you accept and don't accept, what you recognize and don't recognize as the leader. For example, if you allow team members to disrespect and speak negatively of each other, trust and results will diminish. However, if you encourage your team to recognize each other's successes, trust will increase. If you create a "safe" space for team members to speak up, you'll get better ideas! In fact, the bottom-line finding of Google's research was that psychological safety is the most important characteristic of a high-performance team.

It's the kind of environment that Harvard Professor Amy Edmondson describes as: "A sense of confidence that the team will not embarrass, reject, or punish someone for speaking up." (20) This is a climate of mutual respect that encourages people to be themselves, and it is the kind of atmosphere that you can create through your role as a leader. You can create a team that works together to deliver amazing results. It might sound like a tall order, but if you think through the team building process from the beginning, it will seem less daunting.

Leader's Job on Day 1

Sometimes new leaders want to demonstrate that they are firmly in charge and can handle their responsibilities. While such an approach may impress some, perhaps even your boss, it's always a good idea to first understand fully the team's members, its goals, values, and benchmarks for success. Some of the best career advice I've ever received came from a wonderful HR manager at Macy's as I was leaving to take a leadership position at another company. "Don't do anything for thirty days," she advised me after I told her I was anxious to make a difference at my new company. She was so right with that advice. Leaders who begin their job like a raging bull always create a disaster and often never recover from this mistake.

Remember, you are in a minefield of team emotions when you walk in the door. Members will worry about what your arrival will mean for their careers, positions, and the alliances they've built up over time among other team members. Does your arrival mean they will have to "start over?" How can you avoid putting your new employees on edge?

When I ask new managers how they plan to start in their new leadership role, the most frequent answer is something like this: "I'm planning on holding a team meeting so I can tell everyone what is important to me and what I expect." Wrong answer! How would you react to a new boss who began their tenure in this way? Would you appreciate your boss dictating solutions to problems they don't understand on their first day? Probably not. That's why my best advice for Day 1 is to listen, listen, listen! It's fine to have a round of introductions and to answer some questions about your priorities, but stay focused on your mission to better understand your team.

Your goal for the first meeting is to put the team members at ease and lay the first bricks for your foundation of trust. You will do this most effectively by helping each team member to answer these basic questions about you, their new leader:

- Are you likable?
- Will you change things?
- Can I work with you?
- Are you competent?
- Do you have a sense of humor?

Second Step – Understand Your Team

Whether you are leading one person or fifty, take the time to understand each person individually. Although this might sound easy, it is easy to get caught up in your new job and neglect your most important priority—your team. Don't forget: *You cannot get anything done without your team!* Some leaders have admitted to me that they'd been in their jobs for months without even one meeting with their direct reports! While this might sound like an unforgivable oversight, remember that new leaders face a lot of pressure from *their* boss to deliver results sooner rather than later. Still, you absolutely must make time to know your team because delivering results and knowing your team are equal partners in success.

Meeting with Team Members

Meeting with each team member individually as soon as possible will help you to quickly build your relationship and gain understanding that will help you serve your team. The first rule to remember when you start the process of learning about your team members is to do more listening than talking; this is their time to talk, not yours. Since you're the boss there will be plenty of time for them to hear from you. Take advantage of first impressions, and make it a positive one by showing you are a terrific listener. Here are some open-ended questions you might start with:

- What do you want to know?
- What questions do you have?
- What's important to you?
- What are your goals?
- What do you like about your job?
- What are you frustrated about?
- What are you most proud of?
- What are your strengths?
- What do you need to improve?

If you truly listen and make each team member feel comfortable, you'll get invaluable insight into the action and steps you need to take toward the goal of being the Best Boss ever. One note of caution: Most employees will want to turn the conversation to what's important to you. That's fine. Allow the question, but provide your answer at the end of your session. Keep the focus on the team member.

When you do answer questions, answer from a value perspective as discussed earlier in this book. As for questions of business priority, answer definitively if you can, but it's fine to say that you're working to answer this question and that you plan to involve the whole team in the process.

Your First Team Meeting

Once you've met with each individual team member, gather the entire team for a meeting. While your initial meetings provided a culture preview, the first team meeting really does lay the foundation you'll need to create a high-performance team. This next section will help you plan and execute this important first team meeting under three broad agenda item categories: introduction, team guiding principles, and working together.

**Agenda Item #1: Introduction –
Getting to Know Your Team Members**

Even if your team has worked together for a long time, it's important to go through this exercise to build initial trust. Trust is built first on understanding, so ask each person to share as much personal information as you think comfortable or appropriate in your culture. Questions you might use to engage members include:

- Where did you grow up?
- What was unique in your childhood?
- What challenge in your childhood shaped who you are today?
- What do you enjoy most at work?
- What do you think you're particularly good at, that can also help your peers?
- What do you need help with from a business perspective?

This level of sharing, even if it is successful, can be quite awkward. It all depends on the existing level of trust among the team and how comfortable individuals are with sharing this information. But no matter the outcome, structuring your first meeting this way sends a clear message that you are focused on your team and what's important to them.

If you take this approach of putting your team first and understanding their concerns, you will certainly stand out from your peers. Gallup has studied hundreds of organizations to evaluate employee engagement and managerial effectiveness. One of their key findings is that only 18 percent of managers exhibit a high level of talent for managing others. (21) Given that finding, we can assume that 82 percent of managers skip this important information-sharing step and immediately tell their team what they expect them to do!

Agenda Item #2: Guiding Values of the Team

Chapter 2 helped you identify your values as part of a servant leadership model. Now it's your turn to share these values with your team. Resist any urge to share these as "commandments." Rather, do what the best bosses do and involve your team in a values conversation. Of course, it's a risky conversation, especially if your values don't align. But it is better to know about this conflict up front rather than being blindsided by this conflict of values later. Here's a simple road map you can use:

First, share the values of the company (most companies, as we discussed earlier in this book, have a values and/or mission statement). These values are non-negotiable and must be incorporated into your team's conversation about values.

Next, lead your team in a discussion about their own, unique values. Use the list of values we used in Chapter 2 and repeat the same exercise that helped you define your values. Once completed, ask team members to share their top three and say why each value is important to them and why is it important to the company's success.

Finally, share your own top three values with the team. Discuss both the alignment and misalignment of the values identified. Often it is this discussion that begins the process of building team trust as members understand and respect the values held by others. For example, you may find that one member of your team values decisiveness, while another values reflection. By uncovering the potential for clashes between these values (making quick decisions versus contemplating all angles), the team will see the contribution of their peers and identify areas where the team is likely to experience conflict. This discussion is also important to you as the team's leader, both for the cohesion it brings to the team and to gather the vital information needed to be an effective servant leader.

Agenda Item #3: Working Together Effectively

It is your job to establish the ground rules for working together effectively as a team. Often, these rules are unwritten and implicit, but this just leads to confusion and conflict. For example, some teams define "on time" as five minutes early. Other teams define "on time" as arriving within a window of time up to five minutes late. Creating a shared set of expectations will help your team to work together and avoid violating one of these unwritten rules. Establishing these and other basic rules are an essential part of creating a high-performance team governed by a clear set of behaviors and expectations. Once these rules are in place, team members can hold each other accountable which is often a more powerful incentive than any feedback from the boss.

Setting Team Rules

The most meaningful and effective team rules are the ones that the team develops together. Our desire to control our environment is as old as human history. Allowing your team to decide how they will work together gives them a sense of ownership regarding the rules they've created. This approach also ensures that the team will shape their work environment to best suit the unique culture of the team. This exercise is also a terrific way for your team to begin to work together collaboratively. You'll share ideas, resolve conflict, and work together toward a common goal, all behaviors that will be valuable for your team's future success. Here are some guidelines you can use to develop these rules:

Hold a Brainstorm Meeting: Encourage participation from everyone. Remind them to express their ideas freely and that editing of the ideas will come later in the process. Organize your discussion around two topics: *What we do* and *What we don't do*. If you need some questions to begin the conversation, here are some suggestions:

- What do you expect from your peers if you have a disagreement?
- Does everyone need to participate in meetings?
- Is it okay to disagree? If you disagree, must you speak up?
- Who has the authority to make decisions? What decisions can individuals own, what decisions will the team own, and what decisions must involve the boss?
- Is using your phone during meetings okay?
- Is using your laptop during meetings okay?
- How often should we communicate/meet as team?

Sorting It All Out

The discussion will produce a long list, so reducing the list is essential. One of the best ways to pare the list down is to use a simple prioritization exercise. Most leaders facilitate this exercise by recording the suggested rules on a series of whiteboards in a room or simply writing the suggestions on large flip board sheets and taping the sheets to the wall. Once the rules are posted, give each team member five self-adhesive dots, and then tell them to put their dots next to what they believe are the top five rules. The final list of team rules might be something like this:

- We acknowledge each other for our contributions.
- We share talent.
- We all speak up in meetings.
- We don't say negative things about each other.
- We don't miss deadlines.

No matter the final set of rules you develop, this exercise will help you form the basis of a true high-performance team. That's because team members developed the rules collectively and that means a much higher chance that they will engage with them and importantly, follow them. However, be prepared to act when a rule is violated. You are ultimately responsible for the culture of your team, and protecting these team norms is a critical determinant of the team's culture. If you ignore an incident of rule violation, that behavior will continue. If you address the violation with your employee, they will likely adjust their behavior, and you will have protected the strength of your team.

Effective Meetings Build Respectful Culture

One of the most powerful tools you have as a leader is the ability to call a meeting. It's also a tool that is often overused and thus ineffective. Best Bosses respect their team members' time and work to make the best use of this communication and team building tool. What follows are some key points about meetings, including how and when to call them and importantly, how to use them.

Ensure that Something Happens

The worst meetings are those in which nothing changes. If you leave a meeting with no new direction, no new information, or no change in perspective, you've wasted everyone's time. As a leader, you must be ready to engage natural (and productive) conflict that happens when a unique group of people assemble and confront the skills, experience, and perspective of others. Often, nothing happens in a meeting because everyone, including the leader, avoids conflict, sacrificing the idea generation and alignment that comes from honest debate. The leader's role is to ensure this conflict is centered on the issue or problem, and not on individuals. Often, the leader must be willing to put their ideas aside to demonstrate openness to the team's perspective and to allow all members to participate without attempting to align with the boss. This approach creates better solutions with greater alignment to your team's mission and goals, but requires you to listen, not speak. If you're finding this difficult, ask one of your team members to alert you during meetings if you are sharing your opinions too early in the discussion, unintentionally reducing dialogue and discussion. Your discipline in this area will lead to meetings that generate the very best solutions and ideas.

Every Meeting Needs a Purpose

If you can't answer the question, "What will this meeting accomplish?" then cancel the meeting! If your meeting does have a defined purpose, create an agenda to clarify why you've called the meeting and what results you expect at the end. Set timelines for each topic that allow for discussion, but also respect team members' time. It is also important to know your audience and tailor your message accordingly. Leading a group of engineers requires a different communication strategy than a meeting of sales people. When the meeting is over, recap the next steps, including task responsibilities. This simple formula will ensure meetings stay focused on results, not just on talking.

Keep it Short

Most of us hate meetings, so take just the time you need, no more. The biggest applause I ever heard was for the president of a company when he announced the cancellation of recurring meetings. If you want to be the Best Boss, hold fewer meetings, and make them meaningful and as brief as possible.

Encourage Participation

Meetings are a tool to help you create solutions using the combined intelligence and expertise of your team. If your goal is to share information, a meeting is the least efficient method. However, if you want to solve problems, a meeting is a great tool. Harnessing the power of your team will lead to ideas that you would not have created on your own. The key to this power is to make sure everyone participates, and that your meeting is a space where ideas (even seemingly crazy ideas) are heard and considered. Creating this environment will win you the appreciation of your team and give your team the advantage of the best ideas. Make sure everyone speaks up and shares; input from every player will get you the best results. This will require you to both encourage your quieter team members and respectfully silence those that may be dominating discussion.

Two great lines to use are: "Robert, we haven't heard from you yet, what do you think?" and "I believe we've heard everyone's point of view on this topic, let's move on."

One team I worked with identified an opportunity to better surface disagreement. Team members were hesitant to speak up, leading to a lack of honest discussion and the risk of poor solutions that weren't properly vetted. The rule that team developed to increase participation was: "If you don't speak up, we assume you disagree," flipping the normal assumption of silence equating consent. This rule ensured that everyone in the room shared their point of view and led to honest dialogue and better results.

Delegate to Develop Members

Your role as leader doesn't mean you must lead every meeting. Use meetings to develop individual team members by delegating portions of a meeting to a member with a specific ability or knowledge. Not only does the delegation give someone else practice at presenting and facilitating a meeting, it makes meetings more interesting, and team members feel valued.

Start with Recognition

The best meetings start with recognition of team members. The best recognition is specific, sincere, and timely. For example, you might thank a member for reviewing a document for a client meeting and note how helpful their input has been. A team member recognizing another for their help with a project will lead to more collaboration like this. Recognition serves to remind us about what others value and makes that reminder meaningful. In my work with teams, I've found that many leaders are uncomfortable with sincere recognition.

I get it—in our culture we don't normally share openly with others what we appreciate about them. Some leaders think that recognition is not necessary to improve performance; the science on this topic would disagree! Researchers at the National Institute for Psychological Studies in Japan conducted an experiment to determine the impact of praise on performance, using a motor skills task involving tapping out a sequence on a keyboard. The group who received praise following their work performed significantly better on this task the next day. (22) This group of researchers previously found that receiving a compliment activates the same area of the brain (the striatum) as does receiving cash. Let other leaders avoid this powerful tool, and foster recognition if you want to create a culture of collaboration and results

This opening sets the tone for collaboration rather than competition and reinforces established values and culture. Recognition helps you understand team dynamics and communication. For example, if all members participate in this exercise, and team members have good understanding of their respective roles and responsibilities, then you know you're well on your way to building a high-performance team.

"You get what you celebrate."
—*Frank Blake, Former CEO, Home Depot*

Be Creative

If you need to convene your team daily for an update or align around goals, consider a quick "stand-up" meeting. Schedule longer meetings to resolve more difficult or strategic oriented issues to provide time for thoughtful input and reflection. If you want to do long term planning perhaps an offsite meeting with a change of scenery to spark creativity is a good choice.

Once you know the purpose of your meeting, make sure the meeting is structured in the most efficient manner to achieve those goals. Less is more! Your approach to meetings demonstrates your respect for team members' time and the work they do. You will also demonstrate your positive leadership style and free team members up to concentrate on delivering results.

Exercise: Thinking About Meetings

Take a moment to reflect on meetings that you hold. Answer the following questions to create your meeting strategy:

- Are there any meetings that you can eliminate?
- Are there any meetings that you can shorten?
- What do your team members think about your meetings? (If you don't know, ask!)
- Do you adhere to timelines on the agenda while still encouraging participation?
- What is the next meeting you have planned? What is the purpose of that meeting?
- What agenda items can you delegate to your employees?

Write out your agenda with a new approach that will encourage participation and lead to new ideas and solutions.

Handling Conflict

You can count on conflict within your team. While conflict can be positive and lead to better ideas, you can avoid the negative side of unproductive conflict, such as interpersonal conflict, by following these guidelines:

- Address poor performance quickly. Nothing sparks conflict on a work team faster than someone not pulling their weight.
- Set team rules on how to work together. Establishing clear expectations on how the group will resolve differences is a key step.
- Provide clear goals and expectations. Don't leave team members to negotiate their responsibilities.
- Avoid any appearance of favoritism. You'll avoid this outright with clear goals, individual feedback, and recognition to all your associates.

Even with these terrific leadership behaviors, interpersonal conflict will certainly occur. While it is stressful, following these rules will help you resolve the issue, maintain team strength, and maintain your sanity.

Rule #1: Confront the Conflict Directly

If a team member is having a conflict with another member, your first question should be, "Have you spoken with them directly?" Many conflicts are the result of misunderstanding and miscommunication; however, facilitating this face-to-face discussion is often difficult. Encourage your team members to address issues together, and step in to act as mediator if they need assistance. Remember that you are serving as the coach in this situation, not the judge. If you can help your employees to see the other side, treat each other with respect through conflict, and to reach agreement on how to work together, you'll not only have a happier team, you'll teach them a skill that leads to a happier life.

Rule #2: Never Play Favorites

Interpersonal conflict at work often arises from feelings of uncertainty about our role or our job security. Remove this problem by giving your team clear direction, assigned responsibilities, and by going out of your way to treat everyone equally. It is human nature to connect more with some of your associates than with others. If that connection is obvious to the team, it will certainly lead to feelings of mistrust both toward you and toward the associate you value above others. We all want the chance to succeed, so if members feel they cannot trust your objectivity, this lack of trust will express itself through conflict and resistance.

Culture of Favoritism

I've seen a culture of favoritism occur even with managers who are well intentioned and had no idea their staff felt they were unfair. At one point in my career, I worked on a team that was made up entirely of men, except for me. My boss took the entire team (except me) to Hooters for lunch, leaving me to feel clearly out of the group. (I responded by getting promoted from the team, a solution I highly recommend.)

In a true worst-case scenario, a manager of Columbian descent in Miami hired a team that was mostly of Columbian descent as well, even though the surrounding community was largely Cuban. His preference for people of his own ethnic background created intense feelings of mistrust; how could someone of a different background be evaluated fairly when he so obviously held a bias? This is favoritism brought to a level that can create not only conflict, but also serious ethical questions.

One reason favoritism is so dangerous is that it often feels like social rejection. C. Nathan Dewell, PhD, has demonstrated through his research that social rejection not only reduces performance, but it can also lead to aggression, anxiety, depression, and anger. (23) These are certainly not the emotions that will drive great performance on your team! None of us can give our best effort when we're feeling these strong negative emotions. Fostering an environment of belonging may sound "soft"; in actuality, it is critical to enable great results. Avoiding even the slightest appearance of favoritism is critical to your role as the Best Boss.

Rule #3: Keep Your Ear to the Ground

Keep your ear to the ground, and act fast. A Best Boss is the keeper of the culture. You're committed to creating a productive, positive place to work. Be alert for any rumblings of discontent or hidden conflict. You can do this by working alongside your team occasionally, and ask them open-ended questions like these:

- What's working for you here?
- What do you wish was different?
- Who do you go to when you need help?
- What could we do better?
- Is there anyone on the team who needs help?

If you've built trust with your team and kept their confidences, you'll likely hear if conflict is brewing. My advice is to act quickly, and don't wait for it to "blow over." While you wait for an issue to blow over, tensions escalate, and your team is distracted from their goals.

However, acting doesn't necessarily mean that you will solve the problem. You may need to coach an associate on how to handle a difficult conversation, or you may need to adjust your own behavior that is creating a problem (like an impression of favoritism). You'll serve your team by staying cool, avoiding taking sides, and owning up to anything that you've done that has had a negative impact on the team. If you catch these issues early, you'll avoid major blow-ups, keep your team on track, and earn the respect of your team. No drama = no distraction.

Learn from the Best: Advice from Great Leaders

Being a great boss requires commitment not only to your team, but also to your personal growth. Listening to successful leaders accelerates our success by allowing us to learn from their experiences. I've asked the same questions in each of these interviews to demonstrate the many paths to great leadership.

Matt Fenlon, General Manager, MillerCoors

Matt leads the Maryland, D.C., Virginia, and West Virginia markets for MillerCoors. Matt is a passionate advocate for team development and known for delivering exceptional results. Matt's previous positions at MillerCoors include Director, Delhaize Team; Walmart and Sam's Club Chain Sales Manager; Trade Marketing and Distributor Sales Manager. Matt holds a BA from Siena College.

What quality do you think is critical to be a great boss?

While there are quite a few qualities that are critical in terms of leading a team, a few stand out for me:

1. Commitment to development: A development plan should be a true working document, not something that is hidden in a desk drawer. To get to the right culture, and get your team to the right development space, development commitment is critical—in every one-on-one meeting. We want to be both importers and exporters of talent in the company, which means people must want to come work on our team.

2. Clarity of expectations: The *what* is expected of your team and *how* they do their job. Ensuring everybody is on the same page on those expectations is critical for success.

3. Situational leadership: You can't be successful leading a team if you have only one way of leading. You must find out about that employee—what makes them click, what works for them. Sometimes early managers try to impart what they like to their team, and that can backfire. Said more simply—there are individuals who work on my team that are extremely structured, but I am not. I can't help them be successful if I'm not communicating in their style; I'm always mindful of how they work most effectively. Knowing your team members and understanding how they work is really important.

What mistakes do you see new leaders make?

Most new leaders come into a role, and they're able to objectively assess their business or their team. It's easy to identify flaws, or areas to fix, whether that is in approach or process. The biggest mistake I made was to try to fix everything at once. I saw things that were wrong, with business tactics, people, and process. I tried to move us too fast, and my team couldn't execute that level of change. In my drive to improve the business and address opportunities, I moved very quickly, giving my team a lot of messages on changes that needed to occur. I would circle back and find that no action had occurred on that change. I needed to add more follow up to ensure the change I was driving was not only understood but was adopted by my team.

If you had advice for yourself in your first management role, what would it be?

In year two, I really boiled down the executional metrics of the business and identified actionable tactics that we use in every interaction. These tactics are integrated in how we talk about the business, whether in one-on-one meetings, business meetings, or strategy sessions.

When I took on a large business, the sheer volume of work led me to delegate to individuals to accomplish our goals, not to develop those individuals as leaders. I wasn't necessarily mindful of their workload or developmental needs; I was just breaking out the work. This method of delegating wasn't empowering or invigorating for them—they were just doing tasks for me. Once I began delegating based on growth opportunities, my employees not only had the opportunity to develop, but were also more engaged with the work.

What do you think makes a boss great?

Putting your team in front is important. Your team should be celebrated for the wins, and the role of the leader is to push visibility of the team's success upward to leaders in the organization. Great bosses create an empowering environment by supporting their employee's decisions and asking for their input. When this environment exists, nobody is afraid to pick up the phone and challenge or discuss an issue, and everyone contributes ideas to make the business better.

Do you have any secrets for building a great team?

MillerCoors is really focused on building diverse teams. When we think about diversity, it includes diversity of thought and diversity of experience. If there were twenty-eight of me on the team, it would be miserable! I look for people that can bring diversity of all kinds to my team.

I also look for problem solvers. My team is spread geographically and might not see me for four to six weeks, and team members see their peers infrequently. I look for people who can overcome obstacles and deliver results. I look for people who can acknowledge a problem, but quickly move to ways to solve the issue.

How do you stay healthy while doing this job?

I've found that I'm at my best in the morning, and that I need some time during the evening to work out or decompress. This realization led me to set some rules for how I lead my team. For instance, I finish business dinners by seven p.m. so I can get to the gym. I recognize my internal clock and communicate out to my team what my schedule will be; I also empower them to work at times that allow them to perform at their best. Being explicit about working expectations creates clarity and avoids misunderstandings. I don't make my team match my schedule, and I don't feel compelled to answer emails at eleven at night. Ultimately, we own deliverables—I allow my team to do it in the space that works for them.

What advice do you have to address employee performance issues?

My style has been to truly understand. While most companies have processes and tools for performance management, you owe it to your team member and yourself to identify why the employee is struggling. Is it a lack of training, a lack of clarity, a lack of understanding? Step one is to truly understand what that employee needs to go from poor performance to good.

Professional and respectful clarity of expectations create goodwill, even if the employee is not a good fit for the job. Honest and candid conversations can be difficult upfront but make every conversation thereafter easier because the employee is not surprised. Transparency allows the employee to understand what is needed and to have a chance to succeed.

Do you have a favorite interview question that helps you hire great people?

We always do panel interviews for every role. This type of interview provides terrific perspective of thought and helps me to make great hiring decisions. I use situational questions to evaluate a candidate based on their previous performance. A couple of questions I use are:

1. How you differentiate from peers? What did you do differently to get an outcome?

2. Tell me about the most difficult situation you've had to overcome to get a result?

We're all going to go through difficult situations; I'm looking for their approach in their thinking and for their resilience in the face of obstacles. I recommend that managers hire new team members who have the potential to grow at least two jobs higher to create capability for the company. It's tempting to hire just to fill a role, but hiring or promoting is your opportunity to bring in great talent for the future.

What's Next?

One of the biggest challenges facing you as a boss is resolving employee performance issues. Are you confident in your ability to address employees who are performing poorly? Do you dread performance feedback conversations? Would you like to have tools and confidence to deal with poor performance quickly and effectively? In the next chapter, you'll learn how to effectively address employees who are not performing in a way that preserves their dignity or protects your team and your results.

Chapter 6

ADDRESS POOR PERFORMANCE DIRECTLY

IN THIS CHAPTER:
- *Four Steps to Address Performance*
- *When Improvement Efforts Fail*
- *Follow Organizational Policies*
- *Learn from the Best*

The best, and ultimately most respected and successful, bosses deal directly with underperforming employees. This may sound like a simple, common sense admonition for a leader, but unfortunately every leader has a different definition of the word "directly." That's why the notion of "being direct with employees about their performance" may range from debilitating passive aggressive behaviors to vindictive harassment. This chapter, and the one that follows, will help you pursue a more productive path to creating a high-performance team.

Leaders often know based on "gut check" alone that a team member is underperforming. A formal review of relevant performance indicators, such as on time project completion or sales results, just confirms what experience and intuition has already revealed. But no matter how the problem is brought to light, it is the leader's job to deal directly with the problem.

> *"The price of greatness is responsibility."*
> —*Winston Churchill*

Most companies use an established set of policies and procedures designed to help leaders and other managers formally document employee performance along with clear policies and guidelines designed to support performance improvement.

What is offered in this chapter are some baseline, effective, and ethical ways to get non-performing team members back on track or help them transition to a job that's a better fit for their skills and abilities. The steps I suggest will help you steer clear of conflict-avoidant behaviors (cutting off encouragement, interaction, and feedback) until the employee "takes a hint" and leaves on their own. The danger in using these approaches is that the resentful employee you create will likely complain about your behavior to other team members. The negativity distracts other team members and worse, they many begin to question your leadership abilities; i.e., you could end up sinking to WORST boss status. A great relationship with employees is built on trust. If a boss neglects to give honest feedback to employees, she breaks that trust and erodes the relationship with the employee.

Aggressive, hypercritical approaches to improve employee performance are equally destructive and will quickly move you to the WORST boss category. Not only does this behavior destroy any potential avenue for improving an employee's performance, your team will always be worried about becoming the next target of your abuse.

Four Steps to Address Performance Issues

Leaders can avoid over or under reacting to most performance issues by following the four steps outlined below. Note that these steps are grounded in the servant leadership model discussed earlier in this book. Consider what actions a servant leader would take in a comparable situation. Remember, your job is to solve problems, not create new resentments and defensiveness among your team that will ultimately harm your company's productivity.

Step One – Identify gaps in performance

Clearly, your first job is to make sure you understand precisely the performance issue. When you do have a conversation with the employee it is essential that you present a documented case for your performance concerns and an improvement plan that will help the employee get back on track. Here are some areas of inquiry that will help you prepare for this critical conversation:

- **Measurable**
    - o What policy, procedure, or expectation has been violated or not satisfactorily performed by the employee?
    - o Were the expectations/policies/procedures clear?
    - o How often were these expectations not met?

Once you get answers to these questions, you will have clearly defined issues to discuss with the employee.

- **Timely**
  - o Most companies require their managers to provide timely employee feedback and to accurately document when an employee fails to meet performance expectations. Discussing a performance issue that occurred months ago, especially if the issue was not documented appropriately, is not what any employee (or HR department) would call prompt feedback. Discussing such past performance concerns creates resentment and breeds a lack of trust among team members.

- **Comprehensive**
  - o Make sure you and your employee are working toward meeting the same set of expectations, and then make sure your conversation is comprehensive. For example, if you expect team members to treat each other with respect or you have a high standard for customer service, these expectations should be clearly communicated.
  - o Once these expectations are documented, the performance conversation is easier to conduct and will produce better results. It is your job to deal with both the difficult and simple to discuss issues. For example, if an employee is not showing up to work on time and is being disrespectful to other team members and your conversation only addresses timeliness, then the employee

won't have the full information needed to improve. If a boss is too narrow in the definition of the problem, the employee may fix that part of their performance while the bigger issue is unresolved. This scenario creates mistrust and negative feelings, as the employee did what was asked of them, yet the boss is still not happy with performance. The employee in that case is left feeling that the performance management is a personal attack, instead of a sincere partnership to resolve an issue. Avoiding the more difficult issues is tempting but does not serve your employee or your company.

Step Two – Communicate Expectations Clearly With Your Employees

Discussing performance issues with an employee is always a difficult conversation, but as we've discussed it is one of the key responsibilities of a leader. If you've fallen into either the conflict-avoidant or overly critical management trap, as noted above, the conversation will likely be even more difficult. Nevertheless, it is your job as a leader to discuss honestly the performance gaps you have observed and documented. Here's a sample dialogue that poses appropriate questions to ask your employee:

- "Julia, you've been late five times this month. Although we have talked about this on more than one occasion, I am not sure you realize the level of my concern. In fact, you are in danger of losing your job. *What's going on?*"

- "Raquel, I've shared with you the importance of upselling to our business model in our last few meetings. You said you would work harder on this requirement of your job, but according to recent sales reports, you are still having trouble meeting your goals. As you know, this activity is important to the team's success and to your continuing on with the team. How are you feeling about this expectation? What is keeping you from meeting this goal?"
- "Marc, we've discussed our team rule of no backstabbing on several previous occasions. Still, you continue to speak negatively of your peer group and of others in the organization. This is a non-negotiable value for our team and one that must be corrected if you want to remain a member of the team. What's going on?"

You might think these conversations are too direct, but not everyone has your same drive to meet commitments. After all, that's why you were chosen as a leader. You are probably even resilient enough to adapt to poor managers and really do know "how to take a hint." Still, using direct language gets an employee's attention and helps put them on a more productive path and allows you to get back to work leading your team.

Step Three – Get to the Root Cause

Solving employee performance issues means getting to the root cause of the problem. Sometimes, training will solve the problem; other times, the problem may be poor job fit, and the solution may be a job change for the employee. Sometimes, the root cause of a performance issue is a personal problem, such as substance abuse or an unhappy relationship. No matter the circumstance, you cannot really solve the problem without first identifying the root cause. Here are some questions that will help you find the root cause:

- "Why do you feel that way?"
- "What is your understanding of the process?"
- "Why are you doing this job?"
- "What do you love about this job?"
- "What do you hate about this job?"
- "What's going on?"

These questions will elicit answers that allow you to dig deeper. As a leader, you must be prepared to follow the conversation where it leads, even if it's difficult or uncomfortable to do so.

Step Four – Take Action and Gain Commitment

Not every conversation results in the identification of a root cause. Sometimes, an employee cannot articulate why they are struggling in their job; if so, it will be difficult to devise an action plan to help. Still, if you can identify a root cause then you'll need to support your employee's efforts to improve their performance. Generally, closing a performance gap involves answering the following questions:

- Will training close the performance gap?
- If expectations are clearly articulated and understood by the employee, will coaching or mentoring help improve their performance?

- Is the employee motivated to improve? What actions could you, or they, take to increase their motivation? Do they need clear consequences? Do they need additional rewards and recognition to engage fully?
- Is the job the right fit for this employee? Do you see good alignment between your employee's skills and passions and the role? If not, you might need to help them consider alternative roles as part of your plan.

Once you've gained commitment on solutions, set timelines and monitor progress. Remember to recognize improvement, but make sure you continue to insist they meet the standards you've set rather than just make marginal improvements.

When Improvement Efforts Fail

Sometimes, despite all these efforts, your employee's performance does not improve. When this happens, leaders are expected to act decisively. Even though telling an employee they are being "let go" is a difficult conversation, remain supportive, calm, and communicate respectfully. This is harder than it sounds, but here is some guidance you can use to help move the situation to resolution:

- "Jose, we agreed to give your performance a month to see if you could find your passion for selling. You're still not meeting targets, and you've said this might not be the right fit for you. How can I help you transition to a better role for you?"
- "Mark, you've been late to work two more times since our last meeting, without a reason that meets our agreed

upon guidelines. As we've discussed, I'll need to separate your employment. I hope that this may be a new beginning for you, and that you'll be successful in your next job."

- "Stephen, you've gone through re-training, yet you haven't mastered the expectations of this role. What's holding you back? Where do you feel you would be more successful? How can I help you make that move?"

- "Ayanna, your peers have noticed that you've been more positive at work and now look for ways to help the team, recognize their effort, and to resolve conflicts immediately and directly. Thank you for your focus! Let's talk about the next step in your development; what would you like to learn?" (I'll assume that you'll have success turning around performance!)

Follow Organizational Policies

Most organizations have defined policies and procedures to help your organization separate from underperforming employees. Although most companies design these separation rules to be as ethical and fair as possible, separation is also a legal process and certain procedures must be followed.

Ensuring this accountability for your organization is one of your key roles as a leader. Here are some of the most common traps to avoid in the employee separation process:

Waiting too long – The Best Boss never waits to help an employee improve their performance. Ignoring a behavior or mistake implies you approve of it and more importantly, misses an opportunity to help your employee succeed.

Making it personal – Never respond emotionally to a performance issue. While confronting a severely underperforming employee without displaying your frustration is difficult, the result is always a defensive employee. Try to put the performance in perspective by articulating both positive and negative aspects of the employee's performance.

Believing you can fix the issue yourself – Some leaders believe that the success or failure of their employees is a direct reflection on their leadership abilities. This is a fallacy; you can give guidance, feedback, training and even motivation, but we are all ultimately responsible for our own actions and personal growth. Sometimes, more time and effort to fix a performance issue is a waste of time and may ultimately harm the productivity of your team. As Eleanor Roosevelt said, "In the long run, we shape our lives, and we shape ourselves. The process never ends until we die. And the choices we make are ultimately our own responsibility."

Staying a Strong Leader

Having a difficult conversation with an employee who is struggling is not easy, but your team members expect their leader to demonstrate strength, fairness, and compassion. Such behavior lets your team know they can trust you. The plan offered in this chapter will ensure that you are devoting your time to the best performers. Remember, you owe it to your team to ensure that every player is terrific. It's a focus that always builds credibility and trust among your team members and will help differentiate you as the Best Boss for all your employees.

Learn from the Best: Advice from Great Leaders

Being a great boss requires commitment not only to your team, but also to your personal growth. Listening to successful leaders accelerates our success by allowing us to learn from their experiences. I've asked the same questions in each of these interviews to demonstrate the many paths to great leadership.

Shannon Walpole, Senior Counsel, 24 Hour Fitness

Shannon Walpole is a labor and employment attorney, with extensive corporate in-house experience holding senior level positions at both private and public corporations. Shannon has been an eyewitness to the impact of great leadership and to the profound consequences of bad bosses.

What quality do you think is critical to be a great boss?

Integrity, authenticity, and empathy are critical to every success in life. I've seen empathy overused, but recognizing people's humanity and coming from that place makes you successful.

Just because you care doesn't mean you don't hold them accountable; that's not what I'm talking about. Recognize that this is a person, not just a budget line item; a lot of good can come of that. If you fire someone and they understand they were treated fairly, the role just didn't work for them, you'll leave them with their dignity. As a leader, your team must feel that if things go bad, you'll go with them—you'll rise or fall with them.

What mistakes do you see new leaders make?

Confusing leadership with micromanagement and feeling like the way to manage is to control every action instead of developing people.

If you had advice for yourself in your first management role, what would it be?

In my first management role, I didn't have structure. For example, I didn't establish individual touch-base meetings with my associates; I assumed people would come to me when they needed me. I learned that some people were proactive and would communicate with me openly, and others did not. I believed an organic style would work, but I was mistaken. Structure allows all personality types to succeed.

I didn't realize the power of the role and how it impacts others. I know who I am (I'm approachable and kind!) but the role itself is intimidating, and people view you through the role. I would expect normal pushback and disagreement, but people won't do that unless you make it very comfortable for them. People who had worked at this company for twenty-five years feared me! I didn't even contemplate that was possible.

What do you think makes a boss great?

A commitment to their team; a true selfless desire to see each member of your team grow and succeed; being invested in employees' success and development; being willing to give your employees autonomy and space to learn and to fail-forward. You end up with a team everyone wants to be on.

Do you have any secrets for building a great team?

Diversity of thought and approach, because it leads to more robust discussions and more thoughtful, strategic action. It's important because you don't know what you're missing without diversity of thought. Great teams anticipate each other and communicate with and without words –seamless communication. An absence of ego, which starts from the top and comes from a higher purpose of valuing each member of the team. Be demanding, but fair. Be direct; people should know where they stand. Be transparent.

How do you stay healthy while doing this job?

I'm working on mindfulness; staying in the moment. Sometimes a leader will take a crisis and compound it or make it bigger than it is. My mantra is, "No one's gonna die because of this! It's gonna be okay!"

I've realized that my staying up all night worrying will not help the issue. I try not to worry about things I cannot control. Plan for things you can control, and focus on those things you can control.

What advice do you have to address employee performance issues?

I recommend real time, direct feedback and avoiding personalizing the issue. Leaders must manage the employee's performance while keeping their ego intact. Get in the boat with them. Ask, "What can I do to help? What am I doing that's making it difficult for you to achieve this objective?" Keep an open mind as a leader to how you might be contributing to someone's performance issues.

Do you have a favorite interview question that helps you hire great people?

I'm so intuitive, so I go a lot on feel. I ask, "Tell me about yourself." What they focus on speaks volumes. One of the best questions I've been asked is, "Give me an example of a time you failed forward." This requires the candidate to be authentic about their answer, and their willingness to be genuine tells you a lot about them.

Another good question is, "What is something outside of work that you're passionate about?" This question tells a lot about a candidate's action orientation.

What's Next

We've covered how to select exceptional team members, how to create a great culture, and how to deal with poor employee performance. But how do you ensure your team stays on track? The answer is strong talent planning and recruiting. In the next chapter, you'll find tools and techniques to help you build a long-lasting, high-performance team.

Chapter 7

BUILD A HIGH-PERFORMANCE TEAM

IN THIS CHAPTER:
- *Building Bench Strength*
- *When Team Members Leave*
- *Why Diversity is Better*
- *Building the Best Diverse Team*
- *Developing Your Best Talent*
- *Learn from the Best*

The team with the best, most committed and collaborative players wins! It is that simple. The fact is, it's nearly impossible to overcome the drag on your team's performance that one poor player creates. This chapter will help you avoid living through this frustrating, and often career-harming, situation.

I didn't always have such an absolutist position about team members. Early in my career, I thought I was permanently tied to the team I inherited. If my team got in the way of delivering expected results, my fix was to just work harder to make up the difference to meet my goals.

Then one day it dawned on me. I had the team leader's role completely wrong. The leader's job is to CREATE THE BEST team, not MAKE THE BEST of the team you have. It was a liberating revelation. The Best Boss knows: the team with the best players wins!

How to Create the BEST Team

Creating a group of A-team players is a proactive enterprise and will take creativity and energy to make it happen. After all, the best candidates are usually working for someone else, so waiting for an A-team resume to show up in your inbox will likely be a long wait.

The meaning of proactivity varies depending on the industry you're in—i.e., recruitment approaches vary widely between the banking, professional services, and retail industries. If you're in a highly specialized industry, such as financial services or software development, then being proactive will likely mean engaging a professional headhunter to seek out the A-team players.

If you work in the service industry or any other "public facing" industry, such as the restaurant, food and beverage, retail apparel business, or the grocery business, then it's perfectly fine to act as your own recruiting agent as you go about your daily routines. It might seem a presumptuous thing to do, but retail employees are generally flattered when a customer recognizes their exemplary work. If a cashier or sales assistant is especially helpful, enthusiastic, or engaged, passing a business card to them is a very inexpensive recruiting tool; besides, what do you have to lose?

Referrals are another terrific recruitment source to find A-team players, no matter the industry you're in. Call trusted colleagues, ask other team members to suggest potential candidates, and make proper use of social media to seek out candidates. Often a referred candidate is a good match since the person making the referral knows your business and the skills and the knowledge needed to be an A-team player.

> *Band members have a special bond. A great band is more than just some people working together. It's like a highly specialized army unit, or a winning sports team. A unique combination of elements that becomes stronger together than apart.*
> *—Steven Van Zandt*

Using LinkedIn

Using business-focused social media platforms, such as LinkedIn, can also be a valuable recruitment tool. Nearly half a billion people use LinkedIn to connect with their business colleagues, and most participate in special interest groups set up for just about every industry imaginable. However, the powerful platform does have both its strengths and weaknesses. Clearly, a major strength is its reach into all aspects of the business community. The weakness is making effective use of all those thousands of potential connections that could help you find that perfect team member.

One of the most obvious and simple ways to begin using LinkedIn is through an engaging online sales card that will entice the potential team members you want to interview. Here are some basic, but necessary elements to include in your profile:

Your Picture – Fraudsters have occasionally impersonated leaders on LinkedIn, so you'll need to have a picture so potential team members will know you're real; plus, a friendly, inviting photo will certainly help your cause. Make sure your picture is a professional, "great boss" image by following these guidelines:

- Make sure your picture is high quality with great lighting and clarity.
- Use head shots only since the LinkedIn format is small. Photos cropped from larger, full-length pictures won't look great.
- Dress appropriately for your business (no kids, dogs, hamsters, or beer mugs). While the best bosses are approachable, your photo here should communicate that you are a professional.

Recommendations: Recommendations go a long way to make you visible as a Best Boss. You should reach out to trusted colleagues through LinkedIn and ask for these recommendations, even if you feel a bit uncomfortable about asking. The good news is that most of your contacts want to support you and are more than happy to recommend you. Your contacts are probably very busy, so make it easy for them by suggesting a recommendation you've written yourself. This can feel very uncomfortable if you don't like to brag, but you're saving the person recommending you considerable time and energy. Think about what that person would say about you and use that in the recommendation you write. Most people are very happy to recommend you without the associated work of writing the recommendation!

Include a Positive Statement: Create a personal statement about your (and your company's) values and management philosophy. This is a great chance to sell your company and your claim to Best Boss status. Tell prospective team members exactly what you offer: financial incentives, promotion opportunities, more autonomy, a winning team. Remember, you are trying to entice people who are probably happy with their jobs, so you must give them a reason to switch.

Building Bench Strength

Sports teams and businesses live and die on their bench strength. Star players are unlikely to spend their entire careers playing for a single basketball team, just as few A-team members spend their entire careers working for a single employer. What this turnover reality means is that the smart boss is always recruiting and working to keep their bench strong. Recruiting is all about relationship building. A contact you make today may not result in an immediate great hire, but over time you'll reap the rewards when someone you contacted months, or even years, earlier leads to the perfect hire.

For example, I once called a former colleague who I knew would make a terrific vice president for my company. Although he was happy to hear from me, he was not interested in the position because my company's performance at the time worried him. Unfortunately, his facts were correct. However, I told him that I was committed to the success of the business and that I was confident we'd turn things around. It took me about six months to deliver on my promise, and when I asked again, he agreed and eventually made an enormous impact on our business.

Plus, if you are constantly finding potential team members as part of your recruitment process, you'll be able to track the strength of your instincts. Sometimes, that great potential hire turns out to be not so great after all! Proactive recruiting has another benefit; it means you have a backup plan if someone suddenly leaves or is fired, and you need immediate help. Such foresight might also keep you from doing two jobs while you are recruiting for the position you lost. I once asked an audience of leaders if they had ever been forced to take on extra work due to an open position at their company. One hundred percent of the leaders raised their hands! That's an unfortunate situation for both the leader and the team members. The leader is overworked and unable to focus on their job, and team members don't have the full attention of their leader. No winners there. As a leader, it is your responsibility to ensure all your positions are staffed to support both your business and the rest of your team.

When Team Members Leave

Even the Best Boss loses team members, but that loss should not cause major upheaval among your team. To prevent too much drama resulting from a team member's departure, here are some pointers to help you avoid "talent fires," a situation that occurs when a team member:

- Quits
- Is fired, outright for any reason (non-performance or even financial maleficence)
- Relocates
- Is promoted (the best-case scenario!)

The talent fire happens when an open position impacts your business; or you're fearful of firing a non-performing team member because your bench has no replacements; or you suddenly realize that your team is not balanced (i.e., all the team members have the same strengths and weaknesses). Your job as a leader is to prevent these fires from occurring. Here are four steps you can follow to easily avoid the destruction and pain of talent fires:

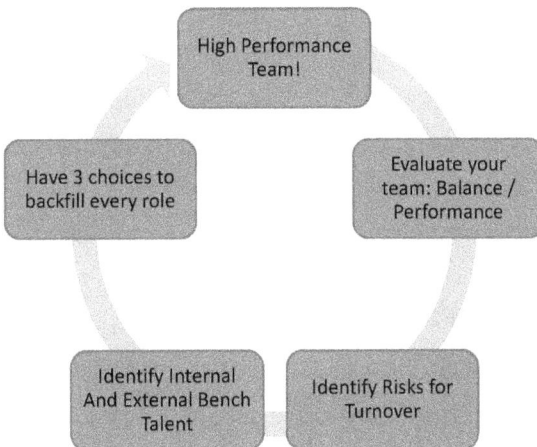

Figure 7.2

Step One – Evaluate your team. Think about the balance of strengths and weaknesses and their overall and individual performance levels—what are you missing?

- **Find any risk for turnover.** Do you have a poor performer? Is anyone retiring? Who is ready for promotion?
- **Be honest with yourself!** Your plan is only as good as your assessment of the risks. If you are unsure about an associate's commitment, or if you want to keep someone on your team, it is a good idea to have a solid plan to replace a member or an enticement to keep a valued member.

Step Two – This is the most critical step! Identify internal and external "bench talent"—nothing is more effective to help you avoid disaster. The time you spend now recruiting talent and identifying internal talent ready for the next job will protect your business and your team. You should identify at least three candidates for each role. Why? Because "stuff" happens such as:

- The perfect candidate fails the background test.
- You uncover a fatal flaw for the candidate in your reference checks.
- Your second choice takes another job offer.

Finding and keeping extraordinary talent is hard work but incredibly important. Always be recruiting! Even if you don't need someone today, I guarantee you'll need someone tomorrow.

Building a Balanced, Diverse Team

A high-performance team is also a balanced team. What are the characteristics of a balanced team? Simply put, a balanced team is not built upon the performance of a lone star performer. Rather, a balanced team is created by ensuring each player brings something valuable to the team that makes it stronger and smarter.

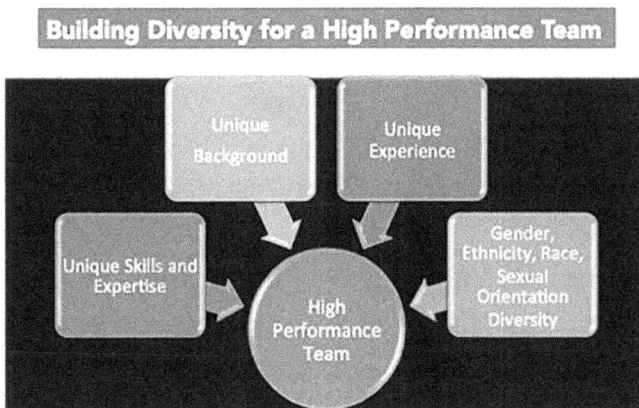

Figure 7.3

Figure 7.3 is a graphic illustration of how to build a diverse, strong team. As the graphic shows, everyone brings something valuable, and all members are a vital piece of the puzzle when you're seeking solutions.

For example, if someone on your team excels at developing and coaching talent, then this member will help you build bench strength. If another team member has a strong ability to work cross-functionally, then your team will have higher performance and a higher profile across the organization. If a team member has talent in building relationships among members, the bonds created will contribute to higher performance. If a team member is a savvy strategic thinker, your team's long-term goals are more likely to be met. If a member is focused on delivering results, then that focus will raise the bar for the entire team.

When building a team, think about the end goal: Your team should help you succeed in every aspect of your business, and only a team with different ideas, perspectives, and experiences will help you reach that goal. If everyone thinks the same, you're missing valuable information.

Why Diversity is Better

McKinsey & Company proved the importance of diverse teams in their 2015 report, "Diversity Matters." The researchers analyzed results from three hundred sixty-six public companies in the U.S., Latin America, United Kingdom, and Canada and found that gender diverse companies are 15 percent more likely to outperform expectations. Significantly, ethnically diverse companies are 35 percent more likely to outperform expectations. (24) The bottom line is that diversity gives you a tremendous advantage in delivering results!

The results of McKinsey's study are also supported by the work of other researchers. Katherine W. Phillips, Professor and Senior Vice Dean at Columbia Business School, has summarized the results of dozens of studies on how diversity impacts work effectiveness. (25) The results of these investigations also show that diversity leads to significantly better business results.

Professor Phillips notes in her study that workplace diversity does create a more difficult communication environment; meaning that we must work harder to ensure understanding in a diverse work environment. However, it is precisely this difficulty that leads us to prepare more thoroughly and work harder to understand alternative ideas. When we work in groups made up of people like us, we often assume we all see things the same way and often move too quickly to consensus. When we work in diverse groups, we consider more ideas, and the outcomes that result are stronger. As Professor Phillips states, "Diversity jolts us into cognitive action in ways that homogeneity simply does not." If you want a team that is smarter and delivers better results, make sure your team is diverse!

Diversity Doesn't Just Happen

Unfortunately, it can be hard to build this diversity, and not because leaders are necessarily racist or sexist. More likely, it's a simple matter of just being human and following old familiar patterns of hiring the people we know or hiring the people known in our networks (both our personal and social media connections). Other, more deeply seated societal factors also make diversity a difficult goal to achieve even when we're fully committed to it.

The clue here is that if you wait for underrepresented candidates to apply you will likely miss out on some extraordinary talent. One way to increase your chances to build diversity is through mentoring underrepresented talent whenever possible and by actively supporting diverse team choices. Overcoming a diversity gap has many benefits beyond just making your team more interesting; it makes your team and your organization more competitive and ultimately more successful!

Building the Best Team

Team leaders who create a truly diverse team and fill their reserve benches with great talent deserve their role as leaders, but even this accomplishment won't guarantee high-performance status. The fact is, diversity and bench strength must be coupled with a truly balanced team that includes a full range of experience levels—the newly promoted, interns, and recent college recruits.

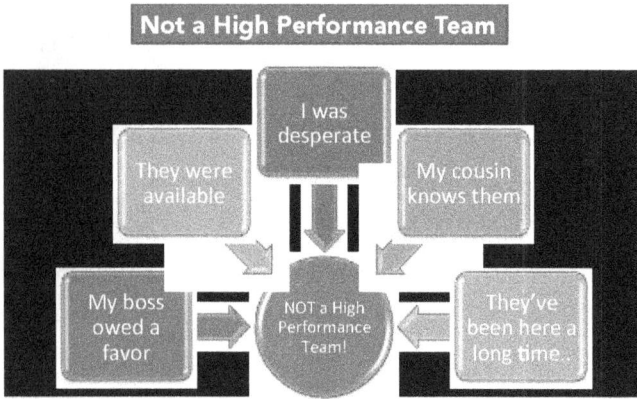

Figure 7.4

If you build a team made up of only those with the highest experience levels, you'll risk future success because the most valuable experience is gained by working on the inside. A truly strong team mixes all aspects of diversity, work history, style, and importantly, experience. Failure to follow this path does not lead to high performance, as shown in Figure 7.4. Clearly, this is not your best choice to succeed.

A Balanced Team

As Figure 7.5 illustrates, a balanced team is perfectly weighted to balance several goals and each element is necessary to deliver consistent, long-term results.

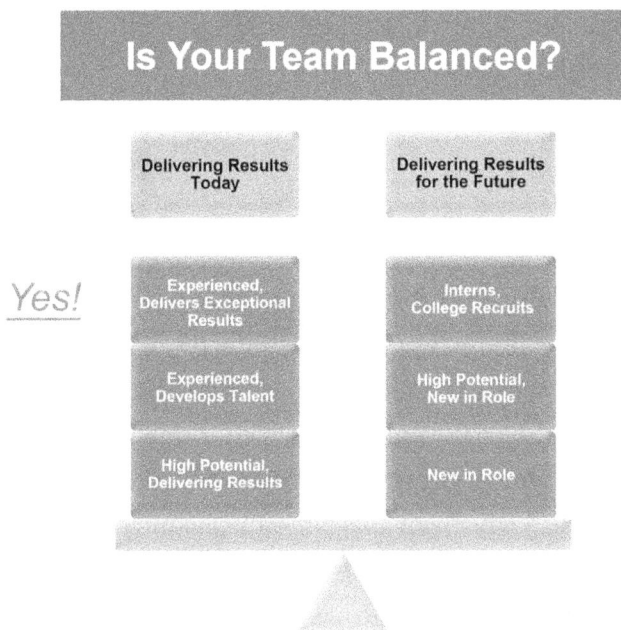

Figure 7.5

Yes, creating this balance takes time and needs a different kind of strategic thinking, but over time it's easy to see why focusing exclusively on today will ultimately fail. Being the Best Boss means that you are providing opportunity for your team. Some of your team members may want to rise through the ranks of your organization; some may be just starting out their careers; and some may value job satisfaction and stability in their current role.

Creating a team with well-balanced experience levels allows every team member to succeed and protects your results. For example, if a team has only members who want to be promoted, your team will lack consistency, and you'll be constantly distracted as those team members move on. If a team has too many "rookies," your performance results will suffer while they learn to do their jobs. If a team has too many people who want to stay in their current position forever, finding a replacement for your own role will be very difficult.

A manager I know delivered terrific results, in large part due to his talented, experienced team. He hired and promoted all his leaders but fought hard to make sure they were never promoted off his team because he feared the impact on his results. That turned out to be a good short-term strategy, but when he was assessed for a promotion he was quickly passed over because he had never developed anyone for promotion. The Best Boss actively works to support their team in their goals, even if those goals mean team members will move on to other roles. This approach will create tremendous loyalty from team members and will give the boss support and partnerships throughout the organization; as their former employees move on to new roles, they will remain grateful for the support and guidance of their Best Boss.

A balanced team creates an environment that allows each member to play a role in advancing the team's progress and results: some members teach, some members learn, some members outperform. Thinking strategically about the balance of team experience is what the Best Boss does; they create a team that provides opportunity and success for all.

Developing Your Best Talent

Team development is one of the key responsibilities of a leader, but which members deserve your development focus? Some leaders believe that helping struggling members is a key responsibility. While that's not an entirely wrong answer, my experience has been that giving time and attention to those doing the best work (and those that have the greatest future potential) greatly increases your team's performance. It might be a counter intuitive notion since these members appear to be doing great without your help. But would it make sense to spend all your time working on products that don't sell? Coaching your top performers to be even better performers is a better use of your time and leads to better results!

Yes, we need to make sure that struggling employees are trained and receive clear direction and feedback. But don't fall into the quicksand of trying to fix everyone! The truth is that you have a lot of power as a leader, but you don't have the power to change everyone into a top performer—these members must develop their own skills along with your support and coaching. Yes, you should create the conditions necessary for improvement, but each of us is ultimately responsible for our own performance and success.

I once endlessly coached individual performers who were lagging and got very poor results for my efforts but eventually learned to prioritize my time and efforts. You should strategically manage team member development time for greatest effect. Figure 7.6 is a graphic illustration of a development decision process that works for me. As you can clearly see, the best potential to drive results is at the front end of the model.

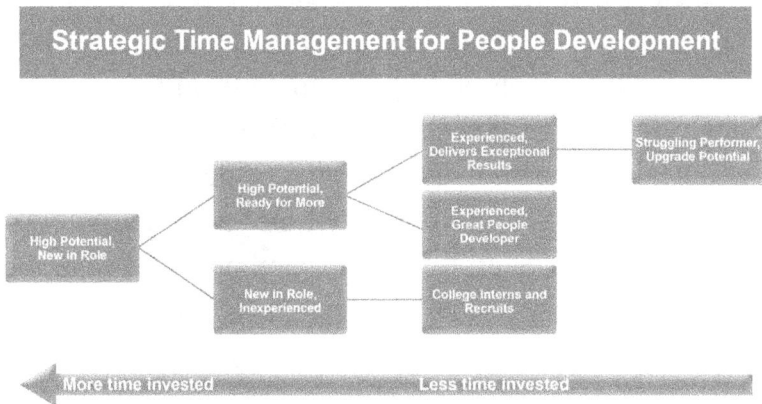

Strategic Time Management for People Development

High Potential, New in Role

High Potential, Ready for More

New in Role, Inexperienced

Experienced, Delivers Exceptional Results

Experienced, Great People Developer

College Interns and Recruits

Struggling Performer, Upgrade Potential

More time invested → Less time invested

Figure 7.6

The model graphically illustrates the reality that leaders do not have unlimited time, so every hour you spend with an employee who is not performing is an hour you cannot spend with your high-potential employee. Where you choose to invest your time is perhaps the most strategic decision you can make! Once we accept the fact that we can't do everything, we can be more thoughtful about where we spend our time.

Note the value of our coaching, even for the employees with the most skill and potential for future leadership roles. Interns or college recruits are also a reliable source of future talent and are a good investment of time and energy by your high-performing employees. Allowing your high-performing employees to coach and develop these rookies helps develop their leadership skills and frees you to focus on higher-level training and development. Everyone wins!

Helping Struggling Members

Clearly, terminating an employee is a very serious decision, and it must be made thoughtfully, but also quickly. An employee who isn't performing not only hinders the team's results, but damages morale. Nothing hurts your credibility as a leader more than allowing an underperforming team member to remain on the team while the rest of the team takes up the slack.

Chapter 6 discussed several ways to help struggling employees get back on track, but sometimes a fix is not possible. You must consider overall team development and ignore any doubt—fear of being disliked, acting too soon, or legal worries. Your action may actually help a struggling employee to find a better job match in your company or another one. Whatever the outcome, your actions and leadership will not only ensure your team delivers terrific results, you'll help the employee move toward personal success. This is the most challenging task of a great boss, and one that requires candor and courage. Your compassionate and assertive leadership in discussing problems will surely set you apart from the competition and set you up as the Best Boss!

Learn from the Best: Advice from Great Leaders

Being a great boss requires commitment not only to your team, but also to your personal growth. Listening to successful leaders accelerates our success by allowing us to learn from their experiences. I've asked the same questions in each of these interviews to demonstrate the many paths to great leadership.

James Clark, President and CEO, Boys & Girls Clubs of America

Jim Clark joined Boys & Girls Clubs of America as president and CEO in January 2012. He leads a network of more than four thousand Boys & Girls Clubs that serve nearly four million young people annually in all fifty states, in large cities and small towns, in public housing and on Native lands, and on U.S. military installations across the globe. More than fifty thousand professional staff members operate the Clubs, supported by some two hundred eighty-five thousand board and program volunteers.

What quality do you think is critical to be a great boss?

I've always tried to take a little bit of each boss I've worked with, either valuable lessons or competencies. Bad bosses helped show me what I didn't want to do! I've found that I've got to be my own self and find my own way. A great boss once told me, "Don't let ego, title, or position take over." Staying true to who you are is key to being a great boss.

A great boss must be a people person. It's the little things that matter and that get you through the difficulties. For example, send everyone a birthday card, with a note telling them what you appreciate about them and their work. It's so easy to get caught up in email and issues and lose focus on people and connections.

What mistakes do you see new leaders make?

Listening: Sometimes new leaders let ego get in their way and believe they are the smartest person in the room.

Communication: As responsibilities go up, you have to remember that you're working on issues together. New leaders often retreat to their own cocoon, missing the opportunity to create a shared vision and goals that will galvanize the team.

Celebration: Leaders often don't take the time to celebrate victories and to continue building relationships.

If you had advice for yourself in your first management role, what would it be?

I was pushed into a senior leadership role at a very young age, leading over fifteen hundred employees as an inexperienced leader. I was probably conflict-avoidant and wanted everyone to be happy. I would tell myself to focus on self-awareness and the importance of being vulnerable. Being vulnerable allows people to know you, see that you are normal, and trust you. I felt like I had to work ten times harder than everyone else; I'd take everything on and was upsetting my team because they didn't feel valued. I would tell myself to give more to them!

What do you think makes a boss great?

A great boss is approachable. You're going to make mistakes, but if you are approachable, people will come and tell you when you do. Approachability builds trust; your people will give you the benefit of the doubt and assume that if you make a mistake, it's not intentional.

A great boss creates an atmosphere conducive to self-motivation. Courage is also important. Leaders have to be willing to make tough decisions and stick to them, and not worry about their popularity. Finally, a relentless pursuit of talent and people development is critical for success.

Do you have any secrets for building a great team?

My success in building a great team is based on my belief in supporting my team in their efforts, not barking out orders. My team sees me as easy to work for, accessible, and ultra-responsive to their needs. I am clear on priorities, but I don't tell them how to get it done. I end every conversation with, "What can I do to help you?"

I treat everyone the same by treating them differently. Everyone wants different ways to be recognized, different kinds of support. Some of my teams like public recognition; others are looking for a quieter focus on the work. Adjusting your approach to fit the needs of the individual leads to everyone feeling valued and supported.

How do you stay healthy while doing this job?

I'm clear on what's important to me: Family comes first. Without a good family life, you won't be successful. I am careful to protect my time with my family, to be there for them, and they notice this commitment. Health is important to success, so I exercise and take care of myself. The success of the kids in our clubs is very important to me and makes it easy to come in early or travel to fulfill our mission. What works for me might not work for you, but if you align your time with your priorities, you'll be successful.

What advice do you have to address employee performance issues?

My advice is to be upfront with clear expectations and active follow-up. There is tremendous value of ongoing conversations on performance instead of waiting for an annual performance review. These conversations save a lot of pain and avoid surprises.

Do you have a favorite interview question or approach to hiring?

I use the behavioral interview style versus engaging in surface level conversation. I go into the interview clear with what I want to find out and tell interviewees that I'm looking for real, not theoretical, examples of what you've done and what was the outcome of your work. I suggest leaders listen to their intuition; it's not the only decision point, but valuable information. If the interview conversation doesn't feel good, it's not going to get better. I only hire people I like!

What's Next

We've covered how to build a high-performance team and how to lead that team to get terrific results. In the next chapter, we'll focus on leading oneself. We'll explore strategies to maximize your time, develop your own leadership, and act as your own Best Boss!

> *"It is necessary to try to surpass one's self always: this occupation ought to last as long as life."*
> —*Queen Christina of Sweden*

Chapter 8

BEING YOUR OWN BEST BOSS

IN THIS CHAPTER:

+ *Working With Your Team*
+ *Moving from Peer to Boss*
+ *Measuring Your Best Boss Performance*
+ *A Growth Mindset*
+ *Finding Time to be the Best Boss*
+ *Leading Yourself to Success*
+ *Learn from the Best*

Some leaders are accidental leaders (promoted based on their expertise, not a desire for leadership). Other leaders recognize early on in their careers that they have a talent (and desire) for leadership and actively pursue achieving that role. However, the one key connection between these two types of leaders is that they both want to be a great boss and achieve success. Unfortunately, what one leader calls exemplary behavior, another leader might call authoritarian and counterproductive.

The fact that you are reading this book tells me you are motivated to be not only an authentic and effective leader, but perhaps even a great leader. You want to deliver results for your organization through the collaborative, productive team you've built through your insistence on mutual respect, setting clear goals, and your strong, but empathetic and principled, leadership style.

Of course, achieving this level of success is not easy and requires sustained commitment and hard work.

Great leaders are constantly striving to learn the craft of leadership. Even the most experienced leaders have room to improve and adapt. Leadership involves people, and people are constantly changing. Leadership requires a commitment to growth, both for ourselves and for our teams. This chapter will help you manage your most important team member—yourself.

Working *With* Your Team

A great boss works *with* and *for* their team. As one new manager told me, "I want my team to know I'm with them... so I do the work as well." That's an approach that will create loyalty and engagement with your team. But remember, if you spend too much time working *with* your team, then is your job being neglected? Yes, working *with* your team does show your commitment, but as we've discussed in this book, you have a different role. It's a leader's job to lead; that means giving your team clearly defined guidance, useful, performance enhancing feedback, coaching and holding members accountable for results. Without your leadership, even the performance of your best employees deteriorates, and the results of your whole team will suffer.

Yes, "getting your hands dirty" and working directly with your team is an effective strategy. But you must be clear about your motivations and the outcomes you want to achieve. Here are some ideas to help you assess when and how to work with your team. You should work with your team to:

- **Build relationships** – Conversation is much easier when you and team members share a task; this creates a terrific opportunity to learn more about your employees' lives outside of work; i.e., what do they do for fun, or what's important to them?
- **Assess performance** – Working alongside a team member gives valuable insight into their knowledge of the job, including their strengths and opportunities for improvement.
- **Be a resource** – Working alongside team members breaks down traditional leader and employee barriers, and it allows team members to seek help or ask questions that might be difficult to pose when sitting across a desk from their boss.

However, "too much of a good thing" can be destructive to you and your team. Some team members might perceive your enthusiasm to work alongside them as micromanagement or inappropriate meddling in their jobs; both perceptions are clear trust destroyers. So, how can you know if you're crossing the line? It's hard to recognize a clear "never cross" boundary, but if you find yourself uttering the following phrases with any great frequency, beware!

- "I'm a very hands-on manager."
- "My team appreciates how hard I work."

- "I need them to know that I'm in it with them."
- "I feel bad asking people to do things when I'm not doing anything."
- "I have the highest productivity on the team."

So how will you know that you've crossed the line between too much "doing" and too little "managing?" As a new manager for one retail store, my boss insisted that I carry a cup of coffee around with me all day as a reminder to resist the urge to "do" instead of lead. Another leader I worked with insisted on never working on a task alone and instead always brought another team member with him so that he could use the time to teach, coach, and build their relationship.

The bottom line to remember is this: Your team wants you to be their leader, and that means trusting them to do their own work. The Best Boss puts their energy toward developing people, setting clear direction, and recognizing the team's wins. The goal is to be the leader, not to be the hardest working person on the team; that's the formula that ultimately leads to team success.

Moving from Peer to Boss

Leaders who make the move from peer to boss on the same team face a difficult challenge. Former peers may have many conflicting emotions about their new boss, including jealousy, excitement, fear, or even anger. Bosses in this situation often make the mistake of trying to live up to their new role with an overbearing approach or go the opposite direction and continue to act like a peer. Either approach guarantees frustration and failure. Here are three tips to make this transition with grace and win your team over quickly:

- **Act the part:** The role of boss carries weight and responsibility. A boss must act differently than a peer, even if that peer is a leader. Actions that are perfectly reasonable as a peer are inappropriate, dangerous, or disrespectful as a boss. For example, peers get together after work over drinks and complain about the job. If a boss joins in, that boss undermines their credibility and undermines trust with the team. Respect your new role, and accept the change from friend to boss by avoiding any activity that might create even the appearance of impropriety. This can be harder than it sounds! Our desire to fit in is powerful and can lead managers to convince themselves that employees can compartmentalize their behavior into "boss time" and "friend time." Unfortunately, as the boss, you are always "on stage"; people will evaluate you tomorrow morning based on what happens tonight. Protect yourself and your reputation by respecting your role enough to act the part.

- **Address the change directly:** Leaders in this situation sometimes neglect meeting one-on-one with employees to discuss the new working relationship, employee goals, and needs. Although you may know someone as a peer, you will now need to understand them as a boss, and that requires a candid and open conversation. Meeting early in your tenure and discussing concerns and expectations for both you and your employee will help avoid unproductive conflict and accelerate your effectiveness. This meeting is the time to ask and answer the uncomfortable questions:

- How do you feel about my promotion?
- What are you worried about in our working relationship?
- How do you think our working relationship will change?
- How can I support you in my new role?

Having the courage to address any underlying tension now will accelerate your effectiveness and reduce your employee's fears, so you can all get to work!

- **Avoid favoritism:** As a peer, you likely confided in, trusted, and just enjoyed some of your team members over others. As we discussed earlier, as a boss, any hint of favoritism is poisonous to team cohesion and employee engagement. Your team will be looking for any indication of favoritism; make extra effort to demonstrate your fairness, and you'll earn the respect of your team.

Many bosses have made this leap from peer to boss. By following the tips above, and the other tactics in this book, you will make that leap successfully, and will quickly earn your Best Boss reputation.

Measuring Your Best Boss Performance
A Growth Mindset

Professor Carol Dweck, of Stanford, has shown through her research that individuals with a "growth mindset" (someone who believes that they can develop their talent through their personal effort) achieve more (26). On the other hand, someone with a fixed mindset (a person who believes that their talents are inherent and cannot be developed) is less likely to achieve, according to Professor Dweck's research. Clearly, your beliefs truly affect your results; if you believe you can improve as a leader (and you work at it!), you will improve. Since we know that leadership skills can be developed, there's no reason that you cannot become an even better boss.

Assessing your own leadership performance is difficult unless your organization has an established manager/leader assessment process that involves your direct reports. Even if you have access to that information, it's a smart idea to engage directly with team members, and ask them to help you gauge your progress. I sometimes find leaders are hesitant to ask their employees for feedback, feeling that this behavior signals weakness. Nothing could be further from the truth! Asking for feedback indicates confidence; people who are insecure never seek out criticism. Soliciting input from your team indicates to them that you value their opinion, and that you care about them and their success. A great boss serves their team members, and in order to serve effectively, you must know how you are doing.

I suggest asking your team members the following questions:

- Do you have the resources you need to achieve your goals?
- How would you rate my availability when you need help?
- What am I doing that you don't think I should be doing?
- How would you rate the team's collaboration?
- How well is the team working together?
- Is there any underlying conflict that is affecting the team?
- What am I doing that is helping you?
- What do you need that you're not getting from me?

Asking these questions quarterly during one-on-one employee meetings provides critical information on what you and your team members can do to improve in your respective jobs. These proactive questions are extremely helpful since they allow for improvement even before learning the results of formal employee assessments (often occurring only annually). Not only will the practice show your openness to learning and feedback—a behavior team members appreciate—you may be able to short circuit negative employee performance feedback during the next company-wide performance review cycle. However, a word of perhaps obvious caution: soliciting your team's opinions about your performance only works if you act! If you don't act, trust will erode, and your opportunity to be a Best Boss will be lost.

> *"Though it's oh so nice to get advice, it's oh so hard to do."*
> *—Joe Jackson, "Breaking Us in Two"*

Exercise: Asking for Feedback

A consistent, thoughtful approach to asking for feedback will build trust with your team and provide the best opportunity for gaining information that will help you grow. Soliciting feedback consistently lays a foundation of trust; your team knows that you value their feedback and encourage them to freely provide it. Take a moment and plan your approach, using these questions as your guide:

- Look at the employee feedback questions above. Which ones resonate with you?
- How will you "check-in" with your team in ways that will keep you on track to be the Best Boss? Will you ask for feedback during one-on-one meetings? How often will you solicit feedback? During every one-on-one? Once a month? Once a quarter?
- Once you've decided, put the "check-in" events on your calendar. Plan these interactions for the entire year. Soliciting feedback isn't easy; committing yourself using your calendar will help you achieve your plan.
- When you get feedback, how will you follow up to make sure you've acted on the feedback? You might consider a thank you note or asking your team member if they've seen a difference during your next few meetings. It's a good idea to follow up a few times to make sure you've made progress and to reinforce the idea that you take feedback seriously.

Managing Your Boss

This book has been focused on your role as the boss and serving your team effectively. You can only do that if you are also serving and managing your boss. The best advice I've ever been given on success came from a store manager at Target when I was fresh out of college. He told me, "If your boss asks you to pick up trash, get it done, get it done quickly, and let them know that you got it done." This simple advice holds even at the highest levels of leadership; giving the boss confidence that important things will get done (whether you think they are important or not) is great for your career whether you are a cashier or the CEO. The other message embedded in this advice is a commitment to humility. Sometimes we need to assume that the boss has a reason for their request and put aside our own priorities to meet that request.

So, what do you do if you disagree with your boss? What if you need something from your boss that you're currently not getting? When should you keep your opinion to yourself, and when should you argue for your point of view? The answers to these questions depend on the situation, and the boss's values, personality, and approach. However, I can offer a few tips based on what I've seen throughout my career and my coaching work. Here are a few rules for success in managing upward:

1. **Assume positive intent:** As a boss yourself, you are keenly aware that the role of boss does not bestow omnipotence, or even competence. It can be tempting to read into a boss's behavior, and assume negative intent, given the tremendous power that bosses carry. I remember one day very early in my career that taught me this lesson. I came in to work that day mentally distracted by all that I had to accomplish and was ruminating on problems to solve the minute I walked into the building. At noon, I noticed one of my employees sitting at her desk, visibly upset. When I asked her what was wrong, she told me that she was sure I was going to fire her, because I hadn't greeted her that morning. The truth is that I hadn't even seen her; I was so preoccupied with my own problems. I did my best after that day to be present and mindful, and to demonstrate to my employees my sincere appreciation. If your boss comes across as rude, uncaring, or disengaged, it's possible they are

stressed, nervous, or overwhelmed. Assuming the most generous possibility will help you avoid making negative assumptions that will prevent you from developing a solid relationship.

2. **Make your ask:** If there is something you need or want from your boss, you gotta ask! In my coaching practice, I've often found that leaders are hesitant to ask the boss for what they need. One common barrier is making assumptions about what is possible, or what the boss will say or do. You simply cannot know what is in someone else's thoughts, and you don't have the same view of the organization and resources that your boss does. If there is something you need—resources, career advice, a raise—you'll never get it if you don't ask. A few tips on asking effectively:

    1. Consider context: Are you asking for budget dollars when the company is in financial straits? Is there an important company goal that you could better support with more headcount? Understanding context will help you frame your request for a better likelihood of success.

    2. Consider setting: If you have an important request or feedback, indicate the importance by the setting. Asking for something by email is only effective if the ask is very easy; it's impossible to effectively overcome objections or convey your strong beliefs over email. Scheduling a meeting with your boss in-person and behind closed doors will get the boss's attention and indicates that this is an important conversation.

3. Consider what's in it for them: Whatever your ask, how does it support your boss? If you get a raise, will you be even more engaged and loyal? If you get an extra headcount added to budget, will you deliver higher sales revenue? If you don't know your boss's goals, get clarity before you make your ask!

3. **Align on your mission:** If you and your team are delivering results on the wrong things, you will absolutely fail. At one point in my career, I led a large group of big-box stores on the East Coast of the U.S. I was a few leadership positions removed from the stores, so I relied on the leaders below me to align the teams on priorities. One day, I walked into a store that had placed diapers right at the front entrance. The team was very excited to share with me their sales on these items—they were selling like crazy. The only problem: the company sold this item at a loss, so every item they sold contributed negative profit. If the team had aligned on the goal of profitable sales vs. sales, we would all have made more money. Clarity on goals and priorities is essential for your success. It is easy to make assumptions about what is important, and these assumptions may be wrong. A best practice is to share your priorities with your boss, and not just at your annual review, but during your weekly one-on-one meetings as well. Business moves very fast, so make sure that your team is working on the right things in order to deliver success.

4. **Accept feedback:** As a boss, you know that sometimes you must deliver feedback that is difficult for your employee to hear. I cringe every time I hear "Feedback

is a gift;" while it may be true, most of us don't want a gift that carries pain and disappointment! Remember that your boss has a different vantage point than you; they may see opportunities that are blind spots for you or see a chance for improvement that you missed. Demonstrate a sincere openness to feedback, and you will gain the insight you need to improve. If you struggle with defensiveness, I recommend this approach when faced with feedback:

1. When given feedback, keep quiet and listen. Ask questions to understand, but don't justify or try to explain yourself.

2. Take a moment to reflect. You can say, "Thank you for this feedback. I need some time to think about what you've told me."

3. Respond to the feedback only after you've had time to think. Where do you find truth in this feedback? Where do you disagree? If you disagree, why might your boss perceive you this way? Most importantly, what will you do differently? Meet again with your boss and share your thoughts on what you will do in the future to address the feedback.

4. Finally, follow up with your boss after a bit of time has passed. Have they seen a difference in your approach? This allows you to make sure you've addressed the issue and also allows you to get credit for the hard work of leadership growth. Taking this approach will allow you to grow, and to keep the channels of communication and feedback open.

5. **Be a confidant:** Assuming positive intent, your boss is doing their best and is hoping for success just as you are. Regardless of personality or style, your boss surely has lessons to teach you about the business and about leadership. You can make the most of this opportunity by asking advice, sharing your ideas, and acting as a confidant for your boss. This may require a shift in your thinking: Your boss is your resource, not your adversary. If you protect conversations with your boss with the most serious confidentiality, and listen with empathy, you will likely be rewarded with good advice and insight that might otherwise not be shared. Finally, it can be lonely being the boss, as you no doubt have experienced. Recognition, when done with sincerity, is very appropriate and also very rarely given upward. Remember, if you want to see more of a behavior, you must recognize that behavior or it may disappear. Recognition for your boss reinforces the behaviors that you value and cements your relationship.

A thoughtful approach to your leader will make you a better leader to your team. Being a great follower is an important task for the Best Boss!

When You Make a Mistake

Yes, *when* you make a mistake, not *if.* The best leaders make mistakes, often on a daily basis. How you handle a mistake has the potential to either demonstrate your integrity or erode trust with your boss and your team. The best approach is to act quickly to acknowledge what has happened and take full

BEING YOUR OWN BEST BOSS

ownership. Over the course of my career, I've seen managers lose their jobs for lying about a mistake, when the mistake itself wouldn't have threatened their livelihood. The temptation to cover-up a mistake is understandable; nobody wants to admit doing something stupid or harmful. However, trying to hide a mistake often turns a minor incident into something major, not to mention the effect on your conscience.

When the Best Boss makes a mistake, the first step is to acknowledge that you screwed up. The second step is to immediately acknowledge it to your own boss, and to explain how you plan to fix the situation. The third step is to apologize to anyone harmed by the mistake. Whether you accidentally sent an email containing salary information to your entire team, or undercharged a customer, your acknowledgement and transparency can save the situation. Of course, mistakes are much less likely to occur when leaders are cool and calm, so let's move on to tactics for strategic time management.

Finding Time to Be the Best Boss

Leaders are paid to think strategically; to focus not only on today's priorities, but those anticipated next week, month, year, or even five years on. The best leaders have mastered the art of working smart, not long. You might be able to judge how you're doing on the "smart" scale (not long and hard), but here are a few questions you might ask to double-check your status:

1. Does your boss often tell you that you're working too hard?
2. Do you often feel burnt out?

3. Does your team delegate work to you?
4. Do you feel that you can't get everything done?
5. Are you working so hard that you're neglecting everyone in your life, including your dog?
6. Are you missing deadlines or rushing to hit a deadline at the last minute?

If you answered yes to any of these questions, you might need some help to become a more productive and successful leader. One excellent way to begin your journey to a well-managed schedule is to create a "time log" to analyze where you're spending your time. Use a paper or electronic calendar divided into thirty-minute segments, and track how you spend your time for an entire week.

Log every activity you do associated with your job at work, and even at home. Make sure you capture everything: the number of phone calls you made and received; the number of emails you sent and received; your social media time; every meeting you attended. Once you've captured this data, carefully analyze the results. What changes can you make so that you can work "smarter" and make better use of your time?

Analyzing Results

How you analyze the results is a personal choice, but it's best if the results are represented visually. For example, if you are analyzing the results on paper, you might use:

- **A red highlighter** to show work that should have been delegated.

- **A blue highlighter** to show work that was necessary and unavoidable (a meeting with your boss).
- **A yellow highlighter** to show email and other administrative work.
- **A green highlighter** to show activity aligned with your goals.

Once you've done this analysis, ask yourself these questions:

- Did I spend enough time reflecting on what's going right in my business and where improvements are needed?

- Did I spend enough time proactively developing my team; i.e., coaching them for growth and success?

- Did I spend enough time planning for the future?

- Did I spend too much time doing work that others could have done? Why?

- Did I spend too much time on tasks that were urgent but not important? How can I avoid those in the future?

- Did I spend too much time on email? How can I limit this activity to give back more time to my team?

- What are my biggest time wasters? What strategies can I use to reduce?

All this analysis will help you get to the root cause of your time problem and point the way to the best solution. I had a coaching client who was a terrific leader but struggled with time management. He was overwhelmed and couldn't complete all he needed to do despite bringing work home and working on weekends. We did an exercise like this and identified that a key issue for him was unplanned interruptions from people wanting to "drop by" and talk to him about problems they were having.

The leader really valued service to others, so this created a real challenge; how could he stop doing something he valued? The leader took several actions that made a difference. First, he enlisted his team's help, asking them to steer problems away from him when he was working on something difficult.

Second, he delegated projects that he had been holding onto to protect his team from the work. This move allowed his team members to grow and develop through more challenging work, while giving him time back on his calendar. Third, he scheduled "office hours" when he would be available for listening to the team. The leader's solution released value back to the team—it allowed him to focus on leadership and development opportunities for other team members—plus, it gave him back his weekends!

The "Never Do" List

Those who achieve Best Boss status have done so by putting in the work needed to create a collaborative, respectful, and efficient work environment. However, those gains are never guaranteed, and that means working equally hard to protect these hard-won results. You can ensure continued success by avoiding these leadership traps:

The Best Boss never...

- Speaks negatively of their employees, the company they work for, or their own boss.
- Sacrifices integrity to get results.
- Forgets that delivering results is the goal.
- Ignores the individual aspirations of their team members.
- Takes credit for the work of others.
- Fails to take ownership of a mistake.

What are your "never" rules?

Leading Yourself to Success

Service focused leaders have a penchant for putting their team, customers, or their company before themselves. However, most successful managers find ways to achieve the right balance between these competing interests that juggle the weight of responsibility and the need to develop healthy, energy-supplying leadership habits. Among the most important of these habits is exercise. Not only does exercise reduce stress, but it also enhances mental and physical health. Sleep is equally important and a critical factor to success. Many great bosses devote time to meditation or prayer, important to calming the stressed mind. Being a great leader is like being a world-class athlete: Your performance will be better if you keep a priority on your mental, physical, and emotional health.

You really can't do everything in a single day, and no amount of worry or stress will add a second to your daily allotment of 1440 minutes. You've got to make choices; the trick is to make choices that align with your goals and values. The good news is that you do have enough time to do what is most important to you! You just have to decide on the things that deserve your "Yes" and the things that warrant your "No" —that's it!

Habits for Success

The pace of business can often derail even the best intentions. The best way to ensure you maintain the practices of a Best Boss is to make the tactics we've covered throughout this book into habits. Daily recognition of your employees, weekly meetings with employees to review progress toward goals, and monthly succession planning are a few terrific habits that will lead to terrific outcomes. Great leaders tend to follow a specific routine that keeps them on track. A few habits of great leaders that lead to success are:

- Morning Organization: Set aside thirty minutes in the morning for your own planning, reflection, and review of the week's goals.

- Evening Recap: Set aside a few minutes at the end of your day for employee recognition, planning for the next day, and catch-up time for any tasks that will keep you up when you're trying to sleep.

- Health Habits: Schedule time for exercise and for any meditation or spiritual practice that's important to you. If family or friends are on your list of values, plan time on your calendar to honor those values. While spontaneity is a nice idea, planning is a more reliable path to achieving your goals.

Making habits of what you want to be doing will help avoid distractions and keep you on track. Finally, a quarterly review will help you evaluate where you are in your growth toward becoming the Best Boss and achieving your personal goals.

Exercise: Quarterly Leadership Reflection

The purpose of this exercise is to align your values and to develop healthy routines and habits.

- Review the values list you made earlier in this book. What is most important to you?

- Review how you spend your time by reviewing the time allocation exercise we did previously in this chapter. Where are your values and your time not aligned?

- Reflect on your health. What habits are serving you well? (Eating, sleeping, exercise, relationships, emotional health)

- Identify two things you could do this quarter to improve your health. How will you protect your commitment to these two activities? Some example options to consider:
    o Set aside time on your calendar for exercise or time with family.
    o Plan meals for the week on the weekend to reduce stress.
    o Schedule time for meditation, reflection, prayer, or time in nature—whatever gives you peace!

     o Use a fitness tracker to keep commitments on track.

     o Plan a reward each week if you stick to your goal.

- Repeat this exercise every quarter for best results!

Learn from the Best: Advice from Great Leaders

Being a great boss requires commitment not only to your team, but also to your personal growth. Listening to successful leaders accelerates our success by allowing us to learn from their experiences. I've asked the same questions in each of these interviews to demonstrate the many paths to great leadership.

Keith White, Executive Vice President of Loss Prevention and Corporate Administration, Gap Inc.

Keith White oversees loss prevention, corporate security, facilities, corporate real estate, corporate services, and business continuity planning for Gap Inc. Under Keith's leadership, Loss Prevention has implemented best-in-class strategies to address loss. Keith has also led the transformation of business continuity planning, setting up a company-wide plan and structure for emergency preparedness and response. With a professional career that spans more than twenty-five years, Keith has also held positions at Target and chairs the Gap Inc. Diversity Council, is the former chairman of the board of directors for the Bay Area American Red Cross Chapter, and is also an advisor and past president to the International Organization of Black Security Executives Board of Directors.

What quality do you think is critical to be a great boss?

The best quality I've seen is empathy. Great bosses are intentional about what they're asking people to do. When you work for a boss who's empathetic, you want to go with whatever they're asking you to do—that commitment is worth its weight in gold. Empathy is the bedrock of a good relationship; the boss understands the effort that may be related to the challenge they're issuing. Sometimes, it's not about if you can do something, it's how you feel about it. Great bosses navigate that emotion to get great execution.

Integrity is so important. When you're courageous with the truth, and you're smart about how you deliver it, people grow to know you as someone who gives their honest opinion, and they'll seek it out. It's a separator—many people mask their opinions and don't share when it can make a difference.

What mistakes do you see new leaders make?

New leaders have a long memory and tend to dwell on the last success or failure. The quicker you can move on the next challenge, the more you'll accomplish. The best quarterbacks throw a touchdown and then come right back and do it again. New leaders can agonize over mistakes and then delay their ability to make the next call. Leaders need to get over it quick and get back in.

Communication is extremely important. Leaders must be quick to inform; I want good news fast, and bad news faster. New leaders struggle with telling others about a mistake, expecting they'll be crushed. The kind of communication I look for in great leaders is not only telling me about the problem but imply that they own it and that it won't happen again. This type of communication really builds trust in the leader's ability.

If you had advice for yourself in your first management role, what would it be?

I would advise myself to be more aggressive and assertive in the business. I knew more than I gave myself credit for and tried to fit in versus leveraging the expertise that was rapidly developing. Press harder, be more confident, and don't be afraid of making mistakes.

What do you think makes a boss great?

Being able to have one foot in the present and another foot in the future. They can understand what's going on today, but they can always give you the vision for two weeks, two years, or ten years from now, so you can see it with them. They get you excited, and you completely buy into the vision. Leaders that articulate the present very well, but they have a clear point of view and vision for the future.

It is important for new leaders to intentionally build relationships and network outside of their pyramid. Learning from other functions about what they do and why it's important increases your business intelligence. Building these relationships gives you people to call when you need help or advice in a difficult situation. New leaders often get busy and don't indulge their intellectual curiosity about other parts of the business. You'll do your job better if you understand the business more fully. The goal is to be seen as a leader, not a leader in a pyramid.

Do you have any secrets for building a great team?

The secret for me is to build my team literally one team member at a time. It's so important to have a team with diversity—the deeper the differences, the better the team. When I've worked with people who have different perspectives, we've achieved better results. Once you find that first team member, make sure the second is different, and the third is different. You're positioning yourself to be prepared for all types of weather the business will bring.

What advice do you have to address employee performance issues?

Leaders must make sure that they are not evaluating performance based on effort and intent. If effort or intent isn't there, then it takes a lot of work to coach forward and up. If effort and intent are present, you can train or help your team member prioritize. When I sleep on a plane, I want my pilot to be both willing and able!

Do you have a favorite interview question that helps you hire great people?

My favorite interview question is: If I was to sit down and talk to someone who worked with you, what would they tell me they liked and didn't like about working with you? I find this question brings out a certain honesty. It also helps me to evaluate a candidate's belief in team service.

You Are Their Best Boss!

You've committed to be the Best Boss. You've built a team with terrific, diverse talent; created excellent values and goals alignment; developed accountability and ways to measure performance; and you now spend your time on the most important priorities (including yourself). Your work has created a high-performance team that exceeds your expectations, and you've improved the community where you work among happier, healthier employees.

You will certainly make mistakes along the way. In fact, if you never make a mistake, you aren't taking enough risks. As a leader, you understand that all failure is an opportunity to learn. Remember, a poor boss responds with frustration and seeks to cast blame for their failures on their team. The Best Boss stops, reflects, and then asks what they can do differently to get back on track. As a Best Boss, you listen more during tough times; you recognize problems more keenly and solve them with more focus. And, importantly, you are confident that your team can rise to any challenge.

The world needs terrific leaders like you who understand the impact they can make in the lives of their team, their companies, and communities. Your positive leadership will have a ripple effect, creating positive outcomes for your employees, their families, friends, and your community. Best Bosses strengthen companies and organizations with engaged, passionate teams that achieve terrific results. The impact you have as a leader is tremendous. Here's to your success!

References:

1. Deloitte 2018 Millennial Survey. https://www2.deloitte.com/global/en/pages/about-deloitte/articles/millennialsurvey.html

2. L.L. Bean Company. https://www.llbean.com/customerService/aboutLLBean/company_values.htmlhttps://www.llbean.com/customerService/aboutLLBean/company_values.html

3. Nordstrom Company Website; https://nordstromcompany-analysis.weebly.com/vission-and-mission.html

4. Life is Good. http://content.lifeisgood.com/purpose/

5. Price, J. and Wolfers, J. "Racial Discrimination Among NBA Referees." *The Quarterly Journal of Economics* 125, no. 4 (2010): 1859-1887.

6. Pope, D., Price, J., and Wolfers, J. "Economic Studies at Brookings: Awareness Reduces Racial Bias." Booth School of Business, University of Chicago. http://www.brookings.edu/~/media/

research/files/papers/2014/02/awareness-reduces-racial-bias/awareness_reduces_racial_bias_wolfers.pdf

7. "100 Best Places to Work." *Fortune Magazine.* http://fortune.com/best-companies/2017/whole-foods-market/

8. "Hiring," Whole Foods. https://careers.wholefoodsmarket.com/global/en/hiring-process

9. Fitzgerald, F. Scott. *Notes from The Last Tycoon.* http://www.notable-quotes.com/f/fitzgerald_f_scott.html

10. Locke, Edwin A., Latham, Gary P., Smith, Ken J., and Wood, Robert E. *A Theory of Goal Setting and Task Performance.* Englewood Cliffs: Prentice Hall College Division, 1990.

11. Locke, Edwin A., Shaw, Karyll N., Saari, Lise M., and Latham, Gary P. "Goal setting and task performance:1969–1980." *Psychological Bulletin* 90, no. 1 (July 1981): 125-152. http://dx.doi.org/10.1037/0033-2909.90.1.125

12. Samuel, Henry. "French Rail Company Order 2,000 Trains Too Wide For Platforms." *The Telegraph.* (May 21, 2014). http://www.telegraph.co.uk/news/worldnews/europe/france/10845789/French-rail-company-order-2000-trains-too-wide-for-platforms.html

13. Cowley, Stacey. "At Wells Fargo, Complaints About Fraudulent Accounts Since 2005." *New York Times.* (October 11, 2016). https://www.nytimes.com/2016/10/12/business/dealbook/at-wells-fargo-complaints-about-fraudulent-accounts-since-2005.html?_r=0

14. Sorenson, Susan. "How Employee Engagement Drives Growth." *Gallup Business Journal.* (June 20, 2013). http://www.gallup. com/businessjournal/163130/employee-engagement-drives-growth.aspx

15. Dewhurst, Martin, Guthridge, Matthew, and Mohr, Elizabeth. "Motivating people: Getting beyond Money." *McKinsey Quarterly.* (November 2009). http://www.mckinsey. com/business-functions/organization/our-insights/ motivating-people-getting-beyond-money

16. Globoforce. Mood Tracker ™ "The Growing Influence of Employee Recognition." Spring 2012. http://www.globoforce.com/ resources/research-reports/mood-tracker-spring-2012-the-growing-influence-of-employee-recognition/

17. SHRM/Globoforce. Employee Recognition Survey: The Business Impact of Employee Recognition. Fall 2012. http://go.globoforce. com/rs/globoforce/images/SHRMFALL2012Survey_web.pdf

18. Duhigg, Charles. "What Google Learned From its Quest To Build The Perfect Team." *The New York Times Magazine.* (February 25, 2016). https://rework.withgoogle.com/blog/ five-keys-to-a-successful-google-team/

19. Rozovsky, Julia. "The Five Keys to a Successful Google Team." November 17, 2005. https://rework.withgoogle.com/blog/ five-keys-to-a-successful-google-team/

20. Edmondson, Amy. "Psychological Safety and Learning Behavior in Work Teams." *Administrative Science Quarterly* 44, no. 2

(June 1999): 350-383. https://sites.fas.harvard.edu/~soc186/
AssignedReadings/Edmondson-Safety.pdf

21. Beck, Randall and Harter, James. "Why good managers are so
    rare." *Harvard Business Review.* (March 13, 2014). https://hbr.
    org/2014/03/why-good-managers-are-so-rare

22. National Institute for Physiological Sciences. "Scientific expla-
    nation to why people perform better after receiving a compli-
    ment." *ScienceDaily.* (November 9, 2012). www.sciencedaily.
    com/releases/2012/11/121109111517.htm

23. Weir, Kristen. "The Pain of Social Rejection." *American
    Psychological Association* 43, no. 4 (April 2012): 50. http://
    www.apa.org/monitor/2012/04/rejection.aspx

24. Hunt, V., Layton, D., and Prince, S. "Why Diversity Matters."
    McKinsey Quarterly (January 2015). http://www.mckin-
    sey.com/business-functions/organization/our-insights/
    why-diversity-matters

25. Phillips, Katherine W. "How Diversity Makes Us Smarter."
    Scientific American (October 1, 2014). http://www.mckin-
    sey.com/business-functions/organization/our-insights/
    why-diversity-matters

26. Dweck, Carol J. *Mindset: The New Psychology of Success.* New
    York: Ballantine Books, 2006.

Your Next Chapter:
Tools and Resources for Your Continued Success

Are you still hungry for more? Here are some of my favorite tools, books, podcasts, and resources that will help you accelerate your growth and success as a leader. Enjoy!

Achieving Your Goals:

The SELF Journal: This is a terrific tool to create focus and consistency toward achieving your goals. The journal is structured to help you identify what you're working toward and where to invest your time every day in pursuit of your most important priorities. You'll be prompted to reflect on your daily successes and opportunities, creating opportunities for personal growth as well as gratitude. You can order from the Best Self Company at https://bestself.co/

Building a High-Performance Team:

The Advantage by Patrick Lencioni: A practical guidebook for leaders who want to capture competitive advantage through an aligned and cohesive team.

The Culture Code by Daniel Coyle: A readable, pragmatic book on creating an incredible team. Mr. Coyle based his book on solid research, backed up by real-life examples and stories.

Making Things Happen:

Exercising Influence by B. Kim Barnes: A real-world approach for effectively influencing others to get more accomplished with less effort.

Be a Kick-Ass Boss Without Losing Your Humanity:

Radical Candor by Kim Scott: This book encourages leaders to care personally and challenge directly to lead teams to phenomenal results.

Podcasts:

The Team Gurus: Mary Walter and Brian Buford
   Inspiring, honest dialogue and reflection on team leadership with real leaders.

What Great Bosses Know: Jill Geisler
   Real world advice for achieving success as a boss.

Dose of Leadership: Former U.S. Marine Richard Rierson
   Educational and inspiring interviews with successful leaders to help fuel your growth.

Coaching for Leaders: Dave Stachowiak
Expert guests and pragmatic advice to improve your leadership.

Manager Tools: Michael Auzenne and Mark Horstman
Advice on everything from interviewing to addressing conflict with your direct reports.

Connect with me!

Let's continue our work together! You can find additional resources, articles, and connect with me at:
http://www.marywalterleadership.com/

Acknowledgements

"At times, our own light goes out and is rekindled by a spark from another person. Each of us has cause to think with deep gratitude of those who have lighted the flame within us."
—*Albert Schweitzer*

My sincerest thanks to the many people who helped me make this book a reality. First and foremost, supreme thanks to all the teams, leaders, and bosses I've worked with through the years. You've given me insight, made me a better boss, and made our work rewarding. Thank you!

My coaching clients: Your growth and commitment inspire me, and you've taught me so much about leadership and how to be a Best Boss. Mark Morrow, my editor: You brought clarity, flexibility, and good humor to this project. Karen and Richard Flanders: My own personal cheerleaders. My friends who believed I could and should write this book, even when I did not: Jacques Herring, Brent Hyder, Brian Buford, Kate Madden-Yee, Mike and Denise Shandroff, B. Kim Barnes, Kelly Marx, Elizabeth Seaton, and all the rest that I'm neglecting to mention but appreciate tremendously!

My dad: for keeping me on track and giving me a gentle nag when I needed it. My mom: for giving me a love of reading. My sisters and nieces: for giving me the gift of laughter and helping me stay young at heart.

Finally, my wonderful husband Patrick and my son Campbell: Your patience, encouragement, and confidence make everything possible.

About the Author

Mary Walter is a leadership coach, speaker, and team effectiveness guru. Mary led teams in retail for over twenty years, holding senior executive positions for Ross Stores, Inc., Gap Inc., Target Corporation, and Macy's. Mary is known for building high-performance, diverse teams who deliver unprecedented financial and customer results. Mary holds an MBA from Northeastern University but says her most important learning has always come from her teams. Mary lives in California with her husband and son.

MWL
Mary Walter Leadership

www.ingramcontent.com/pod-product-compliance
Lightning Source LLC
Chambersburg PA
CBHW071604210326
41597CB00019B/3400